4 1-73

THE PSYCHOANALYTIC YEARS

from

The Collected Works of C. G. Jung

VOLUMES 2, 4, and 17

BOLLINGEN SERIES XX

THE

PSYCHOANALYTIC

YEARS

C. G. JUNG

TRANSLATED BY R. F. C. HULL
AND BY LEOPOLD STEIN IN COLLABORATION
WITH DIANA RIVIERE

BOLLINGEN SERIES

PRINCETON UNIVERSITY PRESS

131.34
J95 p

EDITORIAL NOTE

For some half-dozen years, Jung was to be counted as Freud's leading disciple and, indeed, as the leading psychoanalyst after Freud. The present selection contains the more significant of Jung's shorter writings of that time which demonstrate his position as a Freudian. Before Jung had met Freud, in 1907, he had earned a name in European psychiatry as the leader of experiments with the word-association tests at the Burghölzli Mental Hospital in Zurich. In one of his studies he used psychoanalysis as a method of treatment as well as using psychoanalytic principles in evaluating the test data: "Psychoanalysis and Association Experiments" (1906), which was Jung's first essay on the subject. While the success of this rather experimental demonstration of psychoanalysis may be questioned, Jung's enthusiastic and pioneer use of the technique and his sympathetic concern for the case (of a governess of 37 with a sexual complex) make a decided impression today. Another "pre-Freudian" paper, also from 1906, was a defense—professionally courageous for the time—of Freud's theory of hysteria in reply to criticism by a prominent German neurologist at an international congress. Another paper on the same subject was a report to another congress, in 1908. In 1909, together with Freud and Bleuler, Jung founded the *Jahrbuch für psychoanalytische und psychopathologische Forschungen*, of which he was editor and a frequent contributor. In 1910, he was elected first president of the International Psychoanalytic Association (serving until 1914, nearly two years after his break with Freud). Two of his best known early papers were printed in the yearbook: "The Significance of the Father in the Destiny of the Individual" (1909), which Jung revised in 1948 in order to make its psychoanalytic observations less emphatic (the present version is edited to show both the 1909 and 1948 texts); and "Psychic Conflicts in a Child," given as a lecture at Clark University (Worcester,

v

Mass.) in 1909 and published in the yearbook in 1910 (Jung did not again revise its text but, in 1915, wrote a new foreword in which he stressed different conclusions). Four other brief works of Jung's psychoanalytic phase are also included. By 1912, his deviation from Freud had become evident, but for another two years he called himself a psychoanalyst and continued to write and lecture on "psychoanalysis."

Other Psychoanalytic Writings
"The Analysis of Dreams" (1909), CW 4*
"On the Significance of Number Dreams" (1910), CW 4*
The Freud/Jung Letters (1906–1914)

Transitional Writings
Transformations and Symbols of the Libido (1911–12), translated 1916 by B. M. Hinkle as *Psychology of the Unconscious*, now out of print; in 1952, Jung brought out a thorough-going revision entitled *Symbols of Transformation* (CW 5)
The Theory of Psychoanalysis (1912), CW 4
"New Paths in Psychology" (1912), CW 7†
"General Aspects of Psychoanalysis" (1913), CW 4
"Psychoanalysis and Neurosis" (1913), CW 4
"Crucial Points in Psychoanalysis" (the Jung/Loÿ correspondence, 1914), CW 4

W. M.

* In the Princeton/Bollingen paperback *Dreams*.
† In the Princeton/Bollingen paperback edition of *Two Essays on Analytical Psychology*.

TABLE OF CONTENTS

THE PSYCHOANALYTIC YEARS

PSYCHOANALYSIS AND
ASSOCIATION EXPERIMENTS[1]

660   It is not easy to say in a few words what is the essence of Freud's theory of hysteria and of the psychoanalytic method. Freud's terminology and conceptions are still in the making—luckily, if I may say so, because, in spite of the amazing progress that, thanks to Freud's contributions, insight into hysteria has made in recent years, neither Freud nor we, his followers, have gained full knowledge of it. It is therefore not surprising that Freud in his most recent publication on hysteria[2] has for the most part abandoned the terminology that he had laid down in the *Studies on Hysteria*, and substituted for it a number of different and more fitting expressions. One must understand Freud's terms not as always sharply defined scientific concepts but more as opportune coinages from his rich vocabulary. Anyone writing about Freud should therefore not argue with him about words but rather keep the essential meaning in mind.

661   Freud sees hysteria as caused by and manifesting a series of psychic traumas, culminating at last in a sexual trauma in the prepubertal period. The so-called psychogenic character of hysteria was, of course, already known before Freud. (We have to thank Möbius[3] in particular for a concise definition of the term "psychogenic.") It was known that hysteria stems from ideas marked by the strength of their affect. But it was only Freud who showed us what lines the psychological process follows. He found that the hysterical symptom is essentially a symbol for (fundamentally sexual) ideas that are not present in consciousness but are repressed by strong inhibitions. The repression occurs because these crucial ideas are so charged with painful affects as to make them incompatible with ego-consciousness.

1 [First published in "Psychoanalyse und Assoziationsexperiment," *Journal für Psychologie und Neurologie*, VII (1906): 1–2, 1–24. Republished in *Diagnostische Assoziationsstudien*, Vol. I, pp. 258–81 (VI. Beitrag). Translated by M. D. Eder in *Studies in Word-Association*, pp. 297–321. See supra, par. 1, n. 1.]
2 "Fragment of an Analysis of a Case of Hysteria" (orig. 1905).
3 [Paul Julius Möbius (1853–1907), German neurologist who influenced Freud.]

3

662   The psychoanalytic method is inseparably linked with this conception. It acknowledges the concept of repressed and therefore unconscious ideas. If we inquire from patients about the cause of their illness, we always obtain incorrect or at least incomplete information. If we had been able to get proper information as in, other (physical) diseases, we should already have known a long time ago of the psychogenic nature of hysteria. But this is just the trick of hysteria, that it represses or forgets the real cause, the psychic trauma, and substitutes for it superficial "cover" causes. We often hear from hysterics that their illness stems from a cold, from overwork, from real organic disturbances, etc. And so many doctors are fooled again and again. Others turn to the opposite extreme and allege that all hysterics are liars. So they entirely misunderstand the psychological etiology of hysteria, which actually exists only because ideas incompatible with ego-consciousness have been repressed and can therefore not be reproduced. By means of Freud's psychoanalytic method the barriers between ego-consciousness and repressed ideas are bypassed. This method consists mainly in the patient simply telling spontaneously everything that comes into his mind (Freud called this "free association"). An elaborate description of this method can be found in Freud's book *The Interpretation of Dreams*. Although it is theoretically *a priori* certain that all human ideas are determined, in a most wonderful way, by psychological laws, it is still easy to conceive that an inexperienced person would get lost in the maze of ideas and would finally be hopelessly caught in a blind alley. It is and will remain one of the main objections against the general acceptability of Freud's method that the prerequisite for the practice of psychoanalysis is psychological sensitivity as well as technique, i.e., characteristics that cannot be taken for granted in every physician or psychologist. Then there is a particular way of thinking required for psychoanalysis, which aims at bringing symbols to light. This attitude, however, can only be acquired by constant application. It is a way of thinking that is innate in a poet but is carefully avoided in scientific thought, which is said to be characterized by clear-cut ideas. Thinking in symbols demands from us a new attitude, similar to starting to think in flights of ideas. These seem to be the reasons why Freud's method has only exceptionally been understood and even more rarely

4

practised, so that there are actually only a few authors who appreciate Freud, theoretically or practically (Löwenfeld, Vogt, Bleuler, Warda, Störring, Riklin, Otto Gross, Hellpach).[4]

663 Freud's psychoanalysis is, in spite of the many valuable experiences given to us by its author, still a rather difficult art, since a beginner easily loses courage and orientation when faced with the innumerable obstacles it entails. We lack the security of a framework that would enable us to seek out essential data. Having to search haphazardly in treatment is often tantamount to realizing that one has no idea at what point to tackle the problem.

664 The association experiment has helped us to overcome these first and most important difficulties. As I have shown, particularly in my paper "The Reaction-time Ratio in the Association Experiment,"[5] complexes of ideas referred to as emotionally charged are shown up in the experiment by characteristic disturbances, and their presence and quality can be inferred precisely from these disturbances. This fact is known to be the basis of the "psychological diagnosis of evidence" inaugurated by Wertheimer and Klein,[6] Hans Gross,[7] and Alfred Gross,[8] an apparently not unpromising method of diagnosing from the associations the complex underlying a crime. Everybody, of course, has one or more complexes that manifest themselves in some way in associations. The background of our consciousness (or the unconscious) consists of such complexes. The whole material that can be remembered is grouped around these. They form higher psychic units analogous with the ego-complex.[9] They constellate our whole thinking and acting, therefore also our associations. With the association experiment we always combine a second, which we call the reproduction test.[10] This test consists in making the subject state how he

---

[4] [For Jung's reviews of books by Leopold Löwenfeld and Willy Hellpach, see Vol. 18, *Miscellany*.]

[5] See supra, pars. 602 ff.

[6] Wertheimer, "Experimentelle Untersuchungen zur Tatbestandsdiagnostik" (1905). Wertheimer and Klein, "Psychologische Tatbestandsdiagnostik" (1904).

[7] "Zur psychologischen Tatbestandsdiagnostik" (1905).

[8] "Die Assoziationsmethode in Strafprozess" (1906). Grabowsky, "Psychologische Tatbestandsdiagnostik" (1905).

[9] Bleuler, "Versuch einer naturwissenschaftlichen Betrachtung der psychologischen Grundbegriffe" (1894) and "Consciousness and Association" (orig. 1905).

[10] Jung, "Experimental Observations on the Faculty of Memory," supra.

responded to each stimulus-word in the first test. Where memory fails we usually find a constellation through a complex. The reproduction technique also allows a more detailed description of the complex-disturbances.

665   Every psychogenic neurosis contains a complex that differs from normal complexes by unusually strong emotional charges, and for this reason has such a constellating power that it fetters the whole individual. The complex, therefore, is the *causa morbi* (a certain disposition is, of course, presupposed!). From the associations we can often quickly recognize the nature of the complex, thereby gaining important starting points for causal therapy. A by-product, not to be underestimated, is the increased scientific insight that we obtain into the origin and intrinsic structure of psychogenic neuroses. The essence of these insights has, of course, already been given us long since by Freud, but here he is far too advanced for the understanding of his time. I may therefore be allowed to try to open up new avenues to Freud's body of knowledge. In the papers of the Diagnostic Association Studies published so far, Freud's principles have already been repeatedly used to explain various points. In the present paper I propose to illustrate the connection of psychoanalysis with the association experiment by means of practical examples. I am choosing a common case of obsessional neurosis which I treated in June 1905.

666   Miss. E. came to me for hypnotic treatment of insomnia, which she had had for four months. Besides sleeplessness, she complained of an inner restlessness and excitement, irritability towards her family, impatience and difficulty in getting on with people. Miss E. is 37 years old, a teacher, educated and intelligent, has always been "nervous," has a mentally defective younger sister; father was an alcoholic. Present condition: well nourished, no physical abnormality detectable. Patient makes numerous conspicuously restless and twitching movements. When talking she rarely looks at the doctor, mostly speaks past him, out of the window. Occasionally she turns even further round, often laughs unintentionally, frequently makes a shrugging movement with the shoulder, as if shaking off something repulsive, simultaneously stretching the abdomen forward in a peculiar way.

Her history is very incomplete and vague. One learns that she had been a governess abroad, and was not then ill. The illness started only in recent years and developed gradually to the present

6

climax. She had been treated by various doctors without any success. She now wanted to try hypnosis, but she had to say at once that she was firmly convinced hypnosis would not be successful. Her illness was incurable and she was sure to go mad. She had in any case repeatedly thought that she was not normal, she must already be mad. Here it was obvious that the patient was apparently talking around something that she either did not want to or could not say. On urgent questioning she declared at last, with many defensive movements and persistent blushing, that she certainly could not sleep, because each time she started going off to sleep the thought came that she certainly would not be able to sleep, she would never be able to sleep until she was dead; then she promptly woke up again and could not sleep any more for the rest of the night. Each time she felt tired and again wanted to sleep, a tremendous fear that she would never again be able to sleep until she was mad or dead woke her up afresh. She had a great struggle to bring herself to this explanation, making numerous defensive gestures, which almost gave the impression that she had something sexually indecent to tell and was ashamed of it. Here again the abdominal movements became noticeable. She repeatedly giggled in a coy way. As this gave an inadequate picture of her condition, I was led to ask whether there were any other ideas that tormented her during her sleeplessness. "No, I don't remember anything else—everything is mixed up—oh, there are thousands of things going through my head." She could not, however, produce any of them, made defensive gestures and suddenly said: In any case, she often had such silly thoughts that they actually overcame her and she could not get rid of them whatever efforts she made. She regretted that she could not tell me these thoughts, because she was afraid that I might also be overtaken by such obsessional ideas. Once before she had told a priest and a doctor about some of her thoughts, and she had always had the compulsive idea that she must have infected those people with them, so that they too had obsessional ideas. She had certainly already infected me. I reassured her; I had already heard many such ideas and it had not done me the slightest harm. After this statement she confessed, again with those peculiar defensive gestures, that besides the idea that she had infected the priest and the doctor with obsessional ideas she was tortured by the thought that a woman neighbour who had recently died had, on her account, died without the last sacrament and was having to suffer all the tortures of hell. She had had this idea only since the death; before that she had for several years had the idea that a boy whom she had brought up had afterwards died from the beatings that she had occasionally given him. The fear had tortured her so much that she had twice been obliged to write to the pupil's family to ask how he was. Each time she had done it in quite a casual manner. The good news that she had received on each occasion had calmed her down for the time being, but a few days later the fear was upon her again. This idea had now vanished, but instead she had to blame herself for the death without extreme unction of the neighbour. Her common sense told her that these ideas are nonsense (she said this with a very uncertain voice), but perhaps it was not (she quickly added). Thus she did not correct it completely, but was apparently entirely dominated by the obsessional idea.

The anamnesis did not reveal any sexual abnormalities; i.e., anything that might refer to sexual processes was immediately rejected.

An attempt at hypnosis was frustrated because she could not keep her eyes fixed on anything. In order not to compromise this method from the very beginning by useless trials, I decided first to obtain some information about the psychic material underlying the condition. I therefore carried out the association experiment with her.

1. THE ASSOCIATION EXPERIMENT

667 Here is the whole test:[11]

Stimulus-word	Reaction	Reaction-time (secs.)	Reproduction
1. *head*	*thoughts*	2.2	*hair*
2. green	grass	1.8	+
3. *water*	*drinker, to drink*	2.4	*glass*
4. to prick	needle	3.6	+
5. angel r.	heaven	2.6	+
6. long r.	short	4.0	+
7. ship	sea	1.4	+

668 I cannot give a complete analysis of the associations. In answer to all questions the patient confined herself to saying that nothing special had come to her mind at the critical points. It was thus impossible to find the determinant of the reactions by means of subjective analysis. The objective result of the experiment was, however, sufficient to diagnose the complex, at least in outline, independent of the information given by the patient. I should like to explain in as much detail as possible how I came to this diagnosis.

[11] The incorrectly reproduced associations are in italics. + = correct reproduction. r. = here the patient repeated the stimulus-word quickly in the reaction. One frequently meets this phenomenon in and after complex-reactions.

669 In anticipation, I should mention that the probable mean (Kraepelin) of all the reaction-times of the experiment is 2.4 seconds. This mean is definitely too high for an intelligent and educated person. The mean obtained for twelve educated subjects is 1.5 secs. Since it is mainly emotional influences that prolong the reaction-time,[12] we may infer, from this high figure, a rather strong emotionality in the patient. The reader is asked to keep in mind this figure of 2.4 secs. during the following discussion of the reactions.

670 1, *head / thoughts*, is wrongly reproduced. The complex of the illness may have had an influence here.

671 3, *water / drinker, to drink*, shows a verbal deviation: *drinker* has been corrected to *to drink*. The father was a heavy drinker. The three following reaction-times are all longer than 2.4 secs.; furthermore, there are two stimulus-word repetitions. From *drinker* a perseverating emotional charge may be assumed.[13]

672 5, *angel / heaven*, may have recalled the obsessional idea of the neighbour who died without the sacrament.

8. to plough	to sow	2.2	+
9. *wool*	*to spin*	3.4	—[14]
10. *friendly*	*loving*	3.6	*good*
11. *table*	*woman*	4.6	—
12. to ask	to reply	2.4	+
13. state	church	2.2	+
14. *sulky*	*brave*	1.8	*friendly*
15. stalk	flower	1.8	+

673 What disturbance prolonged the reaction time of *wool* I cannot say. Experience shows that *friendly* (10) very easily produces erotic reminiscences. The remarkable *table / woman* (11), which the patient cannot explain, seems to point to the erotic significance of R. 10. Sensitive people, as all neurotics are, always take stimulus-words personally. It is therefore easy to assume that the patient would like to be the "loving, good woman." That the word *friendly* has a certain tendency to be reproduced becomes apparent from its reappearance in 14.

---

[12] Cf. Jung, "The Reaction-Time Ratio in the Association Experiment," etc.
[13] I cannot deal here with the justification of these inferences. See *ibid.*
[14] — = not reproduced.

9

(Feeling-toned ideas have, of course, a stronger tendency to be reproduced than others.)

16. to dance	to jump	1.8	+
17. lake r.	water	2.4	+
18. ill	healthy	2.0	+
19. pride	haughty	5.0	+
20. to cook	to roast	2.0	+
21. ink	pot	2.0	+
22. *wicked*	*good*	3.0	–
23. needle	prick	2.2	+
24. to swim	water	2.0	+
25. journey	railway	2.2	+
26. blue	red	1.8	+
27. bread	knife	2.0	+
28. *to threaten*	*naughty*	8.0	–

674   *To dance* (16) tends to arouse erotic reminiscences. This assumption is not unjustified here because the following reaction is disturbed.

675   *Ill* (18) and *pride* (19) may easily have been taken personally. *Pride* shows distinct complex-characteristics, *wicked* (22) and *to threaten* (28) obviously aroused feelings too. The response *naughty* to *to threaten* sounds like an association to a child's idea. Has a schoolgirl's reminiscence perhaps been aroused here? *To threaten* can in any case arouse many feeling-toned associations. People with lively complexes are usually somehow afraid of the future. One can therefore often see that they relate *to threaten* to the threatening uncertainty of their future. Naturally, there are often underlying concrete associations as well. One must not forget that a word like *threaten* is seldom used; owing to this "difficulty" it has a somewhat exciting influence; this does not necessarily mean that a complex underlies it. It seems to me wiser, however, to consider the influence of a complex than of a "difficulty." (Cf. Freud's analyses!)

29. lamp	light	1.8	+
30. rich	poor	1.8	+
31. tree	green	1.2	+
32. to sing	to dance	2.0	+
33. pity	poor	2.0	+
34. *yellow*	*flower*	4.2	*green*

35.	mountain r.	work[15]	2.8	+
36.	to play	children	2.2	to dance
37.	salt	bread	2.8	+
38.	new	old	1.6	+

676   *To dance* (16), mentioned in the previous sequence, returns here twice, thus revealing a clear tendency to be reproduced, in accordance with its not inconsiderable emotional charge. In this way frequent repetitions can give away a great deal. A gentleman whom I had asked to be a subject for the experiment was convinced he would not give away any complexes. On the way to me he worked out what he would answer to my stimulus-words; it occurred to him at once that he would say "Paris," a word that seemed to him to have absolutely no personal meaning. True enough, he repeated "Paris" many times during the experiment, declaring this word to be absolutely fortuitous. Six months later he confessed to me that at the time of the test he had still been under the impression of an event that had strongly affected him and which had occurred in Paris. At that time, however, he had thought that Paris had no significance at all for him. I have no reason to doubt this man's truthfulness. *Yellow* (34) certainly had a personal effect, judging from the surrounding complex-disturbances. The patient has a sallow elderly complexion. Women are very sensitive to such things, particularly if an erotic complex is present.

677   That *children* (36) is not reproduced but replaced by another erotic term seems to be worth mentioning.

39.	*habit* r.	*nasty or bad*	12.2	*vicious habit*
40.	to ride r.	to drive	2.4	+
41.	*wall*	*room*	3.0	−
42.	*silly* r.	*clever*	2.8	−
43.	exercise-book	book	3.0	+
44.	*to scorn*	*disdain*	15.2	*to despise*
45.	tooth	abscess	1.4	+

678   In this sequence we meet several serious complex-disturbances. With *habit* (39) and *to scorn* (44), the patient made defensive movements and stamped her foot. An "ugly" or "bad" habit can easily be interpreted in a sexual sense: e.g.,

15 [The association in German seems to have been suggested by *Bergwerk*, 'mine.']

masturbation is a "nasty" habit, a "vicious habit." People indulging in such "vicious habits" are "scorned."

679 *Silly* (42) may be personal or may still belong to the range of the emotional charge perseverating from *habit*. Here her gestures by no means contradict a sexual complex. *Habit* could in some circumstances also mean "the drink habit" and thus have aroused the complex of the drunkard father.

46. correct r.	I should always like to say just the opposite	7.6	incorrect
47. people r.	father	6.0	+
48. to stink	fragrance	4.8	+
49. book r.	pen	4.4	exercise-book
50. unfair r.	sense	3.6	fair
51. frog	green	2.4	+
52. to separate	marriage	2.2	+
53. hunger	thirst	1.4	+
54. white	black	1.8	+

680 If the patient, as we assume, takes the stimulus-words personally and has an erotic complex as indicated, then it is understandable that to *correct* (46) "she would always like to say the opposite," as this fits her behaviour; it also fits the father's dipsomania. Ideas that are determined twice or more do not exclude each other; according to Freud they are even the rule.

681 That *people* (47) is associated with *father* is striking. The reaction seems to be within the field of the emotional charge of *correct*. This could lead to the conclusion that there is some connection, unclear up to now, between her self-reproaches and *father*. (This connection will become clear later on.)

682 What sort of interference acted on *book / pen* (49) is not easy to say. *Book*, pronounced as it is spelled [*Buch*], means "belly" [*Bauch*] in the Swiss dialect. In a sexual complex such an assimilation could easily occur. I have seen it repeatedly in other subjects.

683 The consistent decrease of the reaction-times from *correct*, 7.6 secs., however, indicates a serious complex-interference that begins with this stimulus-word and gradually decreases during the next seven reactions. *Unfair* (50) seems to have been taken personally, and this fits well with her self-recrimination.

55. cattle r.	cow	4.2	+	
56. to attend	disobedient	4.0	+	
57. *pencil*	*to sharpen*	3.0	*pointed*	
58. dull	weather	1.8	+	
59. plum	tree	3.8	+	
60. to meet	certain	1.4	+	
61. law	state	2.8	+	
62. *dear*	*good*	4.0	*child*	
63. glass	wa-water	1.6	+	
64. *to quarrel*	*argument*	2.4	*discord*	
65. *goat*	*milk*	2.0	*to milk*	

684   I have no explanation for the disturbance at 55, *cattle. Disobedient* (56) reminds one of the previous *naughty*, which may be related to the pupil already mentioned. The disturbance of the following unrelated reaction indicates the perseverating emotional charge. R.59, *plum / tree*, does not seem to have passed by smoothly, judging by the length of the reaction-time. The word here used for *plum* is not an everyday word; it is, however, unlikely that for this reason it takes an educated subject such a long time to react. (Wehrlin's idiots have average figures varying between 3.0 secs. and 37 secs. Therefore 3.8 seems far too long for an educated person.) The German *Pflaume* (plum) is, like Swiss *Zwetschge* (plum), a popular sex-symbol in our colloquial language.

685   *Dear* (62) can easily indicate an erotic complex. At *glass* (63) the complex of the dipsomaniac father apparently comes to the surface again with the strong emotional charge attached to it (hence the disturbance of the two following reactions).

66. large	small	2.6	+	
67. potato r.	floury	6.0	+	
68. to grind	mill	2.0	+	
69. part r.	small	11.6	+	
70. *old*	*ugly*	3.0	*young, un-* *attractive*	
71. *flower*	*beautiful*	2.0	*scent*	
72. *to beat*	*rod*	2.8	—	
73. cupboard	table	2.8	+	

686   *Large* (66) is as a rule taken personally. The patient is very short. With an erotic complex, she is, as we have already seen,

bound to be much concerned with her body. This might explain the disturbance of the following reaction.

687   For *part* (69), the reaction-time is very much extended. It is usual to interpret "part" as "genital." Here the strong emotional charge is characteristic for this association. It is not surprising under this constellation that *old* (70) is given a personal erotic meaning. How strongly emphasized in this patient is the question of physical beauty and her own ageing can be seen from the perseveration *beautiful* (71). *To beat / rod* (72) can again have been specially constellated by the obsessional idea that she had caused her pupil's death.

74. wild	child	2.4	+
75. family	large	2.4	+
76. to wash r.	to clean	3.0	+
77. cow	to milk	1.8	+
78. stranger	nostalgia	14.8	+
79. happiness r.	unhappiness	3.0	+
80. to tell	story	1.6	+

688   The minor disturbance at 76, *to wash*, can be explained by the preceding erotic concepts *child* and *family*. *Stranger* (78) apparently aroused a personal association, to be explained later on.

81. propriety	intellect	4.6	+
82. narrow r.	small	3.2	+
83. brother	sister	1.0	+
84. damage r.	neighbour	4.0	+
85. stork r.	church	2.4	+
86. false r.	unfaithful	3.0	+
87. fear	anxiety	2.4	+
88. to kiss	mouth	2.2	+
89. fire	blaze	1.8	+
90. dirty	sticky	2.2	+
91. door	fold	1.6	+

689   The sound association of 81, *propriety / intellect* (*Anstand / Verstand*) is most striking. Let us remember the disturbances produced by *habit*! There we suspected the "vicious habit" of masturbation. Here too this complex could have been aroused. In this case *intellect* is not fortuitous. According to a

popular belief masturbation destroys the reason, the "intellect." One has also to bear in mind the patient's bemoaning that she is afraid of losing her reason.

690   *Narrow / small* (82) is still under the influence of the preceding reaction: *small* probably belongs to the body-complex in view of its being repeated (66); *narrow* may, under the constellation of the preceding association, refer to the *introitus vaginae* and therefore be connected with *small*, which indicates her figure; the ominous "part" too is *small* (this assumption will be confirmed). *Damage* (84) is probably taken personally; *neighbour* fits neatly. She has done immense damage to the neighbour by being guilty of her dying unabsolved. Under the sexual constellation, however, "damage" can also have been taken personally; one does personal and mental damage to oneself by masturbation (see above). The neighbour then provides a cover (see Freud's similar conclusions). Behind the neighbour the patient herself may be hidden. That an emotional charge interfered here becomes apparent from the following disturbances. At 86, *false / unfaithful,* a definite erotic reminiscence can easily have come to the surface in an elderly spinster.

92. to choose r.	teacher	4.4	+
93. hay	straw	1.8	+
94. *still*	*stool*	13.0	*child*
95. mockery	scorn	1.4	+
96. to sleep r.	to wake	3.4	+
97. month	year	1.6	+
98. coloured	gaudy	2.4	+
99. dog	cat	1.2	+
100. to talk	to be silent	1.4	+

691   To *to choose* (92) women like to associate the thought of marriage.

692   The patient's father was a teacher. She is a teacher. It would be easy to assume that she has marriage with a teacher in mind. The father-complex may, however, also have to be considered here (see below). *Still / stool* (94) is a striking sound association. The explanation is given by the erotically charged term *child.* A child can be "still"; but the dead are also still (obsessive idea: she has caused the pupil's death by ill-treating him). Behind this there may be erotic connections, associated

with German "stillen" (to suckle). (Cf. 49, *book*, and subsequent comment.) The same word (*stillen*) can be used for quieting a child or quieting sexual desire. *To sleep* (96) has many erotic associations. The patient cannot sleep, for instance; sleeplessness in younger people, however, is often the expression of lack of sexual satisfaction (Freud). Anyone inexperienced in the field of pathological association psychology will probably shake his head at the above suppositions; he will perhaps see in them not just hypotheses but sheer phantasms. The judgment on them will perhaps be the same as on Freud's *Interpretation of Dreams.*

693   Let us next summarize the result of the association and reproduction test. As I have already said, the patient did not give any information about herself; I am therefore entirely dependent on the objective data of the test and on my experience.

694   The probable mean of the reaction-times is 2.4 secs. Fortyfour per cent of the reaction-times exceed 2.4 secs. Amongst these are figures of up to 15.2 secs., pointing to the dominance of emotion or, in other words, a considerable lack of control of the psychic material.

695   In the analysis we indicated the existence of various complexes. The erotic complex appears to play a dominant role. Here I give a tabulated survey of the complex-reactions. The following examples should be understood as related to an erotic complex:[16]

10.	*friendly*	*loving*	3.6	*good*
11.	*table*	*woman*	4.6	—
12.			2.4	
13.			2.2	
14.			1.8	
16.	to dance	to jump	1.8	+
17.	lake r.	water	2.4	+
34.	*yellow*	*flower*	4.2	*green*
35.	mountain r.	work[17]	2.8	+
36.			2.2	

[16] In order to set the complex-disturbances in relief, I am adding all the perseveration phenomena and also the gradually decreasing times of the subsequent reactions.

[17] [See supra, n. 15.]

39. *habit* r.	*nasty or bad*	12.2	*vicious habit*
40. to ride r.	to drive	2.4	+
41. *wall*	*room*	3.0	—
44. *to scorn*	*disdain*	15.2	*to despise*
45.		1.4	
59. plum	tree	3.8	+
62. *dear*	*good*	4.0	*child*
66. large	small	2.6	+
67. potato r.	floury	6.0	+
68.		2.0	
69. part r.	small	11.6	—
70. *old*	*ugly*	3.0	*young, un-attractive*
71. *flower*	*beautiful*	2.0	*scent*
72. *to beat*	*rod*	2.8	—
73.		2.8	
74. wild	child	2.4	+
75. family	large	2.4	+
76. to wash r.	to clean	3.0	+
81. propriety	intellect	4.6	+
82. narrow r.	small	3.2	+
83.		1.0	
86. false r.	unfaithful	3.0	+
87.		2.4	
88.		2.2	
89.		1.8	
92. to choose r.	teacher	4.4	+
93.		1.8	
94. *still*	*stool*	13.0	*child*
95.		1.4	
96. to sleep r.	to wake	3.4	+
97.		1.6	

696   These associations, which presumably have a sexual background and which show all the characteristic complex-disturbances, could be interpreted as follows:

697   The patient feels herself to be old and ugly, is very sensitive about her sallow complexion, above all pays anxious attention to her body; in particular she does not like being so small. Presumably she has a great desire to get married; she would certainly be a loving wife to her husband and she would like to have children. Behind these not very suspicious erotic symptoms, however, there seems to lie a sexual complex that the

patient has every reason to repress. There are signs that allow the conclusion that she pays more than usual attention to her genitals. In a well brought-up and educated woman this can only refer to masturbation; masturbation, however, in the wider sense of a perverse self-satisfaction.

698   Masturbation is one of the most frequent sources of self-reproach[18] and self-criticism. This complex, or, better, this aspect of the sexual complex, is also indicated by the following associations:

14. *sulky*	*brave*	1.8	*friendly*
19. pride	haughty	5.0	+
22. *wicked*	*good*	3.0	—
23.		2.2	
24.		2.0	
42. *silly* r.	*clever*	2.8	—
43. exercise-book	book	3.0	+
46. *correct* r.	*I should always like to say just the opposite*	7.6	*incorrect*
47. people r.	father	6.0	+
48. to stink	fragrance	4.8	+
49. *book* r.	*pen*	4.4	*exercise-book*
50. *unfair* r.	*sense*	3.6	*fair*
51.		2.4	
52.		2.2	
53.		1.4	

699   To the complex of the alcoholic father can be related:

3. *water*	*drinker, to drink*	2.4	*glass*
4.		3.6	
63. glass	wa-water	1.6	+
64. *to quarrel*	*argument*	2.4	*discord*
65. *goat*	*milk*	2.0	*to milk*

700   From this tabulation it can be seen that the sexual complex is well in the foreground. Although, as I have already mentioned, a direct confirmation of this interpretation was not to be had from the patient, I took the complex-diagnosis as confirmed for the reasons I have just given.

[18] The reproaches are originally restricted to the sexual complex but, according to our experience, are soon applied to a wider field.

701 I told her therefore that I was sure her obsessional ideas were nothing but excuses and shiftings, that in reality she was tortured by sexual ideas.

702 The patient denied this explanation with affect and sincere conviction. Had I not been convinced through the association experiment of the existence of a particularly marked sexual complex, my certainty would probably have been shaken. I appealed to her intelligence and truthfulness: she assured me that if she knew of anything of the kind she would tell me, because she well knew it would be silly to conceal such thoughts from the doctor. She had thought of getting married, "as everyone else did, but not more." After this I let the patient go and asked her to come again in two days' time.

2. PSYCHOANALYSIS

703 For psychoanalysis the patient's mental condition is important, but still more important is the mental condition of the doctor. Here probably lies the secret of why Freud's psychoanalysis is disregarded by the world of science. He who approaches a case with anything but absolute conviction is soon lost in the snares and traps laid by the complex of hysterical illness at whatever point he hopes to take hold of it. One has to know from the very beginning that everything in the hysteric is trying to prevent an exploration of the complex. Where necessary, not only the patient's interest and his regard for the doctor fail, but also his thinking, memory, and finally even his language. But precisely these peculiar defence-mechanisms give the complex away.

704 Just as hesitating, faulty reproduction and all the other characteristic disturbances always occur in the association experiment whenever the complex is touched on, so in the analysis difficulties always arise whenever one gets close to the complex. In order to bypass these difficulties, Freud, as is well known, induces "free associations." It is a very simple method and one has only to practice it for some little time to become reasonably familiar with it. In this case I carried out psychoanalysis strictly on Freud's lines. I made the patient take an easy-chair and sat down behind her, so as not to confuse her. Then I asked her to tell me calmly everything that came into her mind, no matter what it was about. The patient laughed;

surely one could not say every piece of nonsense that came into one's mind. But I adhered to my request. Then she tried several times to say something, suppressed it, however, each time with the excuse that it was silly—I would laugh at her and think she was an ungrateful person who could only offer banalities. I did nothing but encourage her to continue to talk and eventually the patient produced the following sentences: "I think I shall never get well—now you are sure to laugh— but I am convinced that I shall never get well—you cannot hypnotize me—you will no more cure me than any other doctor has—it will only get worse, because now I have to reproach myself that with my nonsense I am only unnecessarily wasting your time." This idea was not quite unjustified because the patient always blurted out the sentences after long intervals, so that it took us almost half an hour to come to this meagre result. She continued: "I am thinking now of my people at home, how hard they work and how they need me; while I am here, good for nothing but my silly ideas—you too will certainly become infected by them—now I am thinking that I cannot sleep, that last night I took 1 g. of Veronal, although you have forbidden it—I am sure I shall never be able to sleep. How can you expect to cure me?—What do you want me to tell you? [Here a certain restlessness became noticeable.] But I cannot tell you every piece of nonsense that comes into my head. [Increasing restlessness, shrugging of the shoulders, makes stamping movements with her foot now and then, shakes herself as if in great indignation.] No, this is nonsense—I don't know of anything else now—really, I don't know of anything else. [Very restless, wriggles and turns in her chair, makes defensive movements by shaking her thorax to and fro and makes elbow movements as if pushing something away.] At last she jumps up and wants to go, she cannot think of anything else at all! With gentle force I make her sit down in the chair and remind her that as she has come to me to be cured, she must follow my directions. After a long debate on the use and purpose of my method, she at last consents to stay and continue, but soon the movements of indignation and defence are resumed, she literally wriggles in the chair; occasionally she straightens herself with a forcible movement, as if she had come to a decision after the greatest struggle with herself. At last she says meekly: "Oh, something silly came into my head—you are sure to laugh—but you must not tell anybody else—it is really nothing—it is something quite simple—no, I can't tell you, never—it has nothing at all to do with my illness—I am only wasting your time with it—really, it doesn't mean anything at all—have I really got to tell it? Do you really insist on it? Oh, well, I may as well tell you, then I shall be rid of it. Well,— once I was in France—no, it's impossible, and if I have to sit in this chair for another four weeks [with sudden determination] well, I was a governess in France—there was also a maidservant—no, no, I cannot tell it—no, there was a gardener— for goodness sake, what will you think of me? This is really sheer torture—I have certainly never thought of such a thing!"

705   Between these painful ejaculations the following story at last emerged with innumerable stoppages and many interruptions, during which she asserted that this was the first and last session with me.

706   Her employer also had a gardener, who once said to her that he would like to sleep with her. While saying this he tried to kiss her, but the patient pushed him away. When she went to bed that evening she listened at the door and wondered what it would be like if he did come to sleep with her; then a frantic fear overtook her that he might really come. Once in bed she was still compelled to think of what it would be like if he came, then reproached herself anew for thinking such things. The thought of what it would be like to sleep with the gardener did not, however, leave her, although she was again and again shocked at finding herself capable of such thoughts. In this mental turmoil she was unable to get to sleep until the morning.

707   The first session took no less than an hour and a half. Its result was a sexual history! What was particularly interesting to me was its quite spontaneous appearance with the same gestures that I had immediately noticed in the patient at the first consultation. These tic-like phenomena had a very close and easily understandable connection with the repressed sexual matters! I arranged the following session for two days later, which was at once accepted, the patient looking very relieved and not saying another word about leaving.

708   On the day of the appointment I was busy with some urgent work when the patient came and therefore sent her a message, asking her to come in the evening instead. She, however, sent the reply that she could not possibly wait, she had to speak to me urgently. I thought something special had happened and went to her. I found her in great distress: she had not slept at all, not a minute, she had had to take drugs again, etc. I asked her whether she had been brooding again over her obsessional ideas: "No, something much worse; now I have my head full of that nonsense that I told you about last time. Now I can think only of these stories and therefore cannot close an eye; because of them I toss and turn all night long and cannot get rid of these thoughts for a minute. I have definitely got to talk to you now; it gives me no peace." She went on to tell me that last time she had gone home very much relieved and calmed down, almost in a gay mood, and had hoped she would now at last be able to sleep, but then a story came into her mind that she should have told me last time, but which she had thought was not really of any importance. She had determined now not to "act so silly" as last time, but freely to tell everything she thought of. Then the confession would soon be over. So I resumed the analysis, hoping it would go off smoothly without the endless preliminaries of the time before. I was, however, completely mistaken. The patient repeated the interjections of the first session almost verbatim. After an hour and a half of mental torture I brought the following story to light: In the same house where the patient was a governess, there was also a maid[19] who had a lover, with whom she had sexual intercourse. This girl had also had sexual intercourse with the gardener. The patient often discussed sexual topics with her and in particular the sex life of master and mistress. The patient and the maid even investigated their beds for sperm stains and other signs of sexual intercourse! Every time, after such amusements, the patient suffered the severest self-reproaches on her indecency and spent sleepless nights, during which she turned and tossed about because of torturing reproaches and voluptuous fantasies.

19 Cf. the reference to this maid in the first session.

709   When, after tiresome resistance, the story was out at last, the patient declared: now she had come to the end, this was all, nothing else came to her mind now. If only she could sleep; the telling of these stories did not help at all.

710   Two days later she came to the third session and said: After the previous session she had been rather quiet again, but as soon as she was in bed at night another new story had come to her mind which had tortured her incessantly, with the obsessive reproach that again she had not told me everything in the session. She was sure now that today she could tell me the story quickly, without the continuous resistance as in the first two sessions. The third one, however, proceeded exactly in the same way as the two previous ones: incessant interjections, excuses, etc. Particularly conspicuous was the tendency to present the matter as perfectly natural, as if there was nothing to it. It was about a second maid who was in service with the same employer. The master had a valet who pursued the girl. He did not, however, succeed in seducing her. At last, one evening, when there was a party in the house, he managed to entice the girl into the garden. The couple was, however, surprised by the mistress at the critical moment. At this the youth is said to have exclaimed: What a pity, he was just ready! The patient heard this story from the first maid. At first she made out not to have the slightest interest in the story, as if she found it downright repulsive. This, however, had been a lie, because in fact she had had the greatest interest in it; she had several times tried to bring the maid back to this topic in order to hear every detail. At night she had hardly been able to sleep from curiosity, and had incessantly had to ask herself the questions: What did the two want in the garden? In what posture could they have been found by the mistress? What had the youth been ready for? What would have happened if the mistress had not come? Although she knew the answers perfectly well, she could not stop asking herself these questions over and over again. At last she was compelled to think over persistently what she would have done in such a situation. This excitement lasted for several days.

711   We have mentioned being struck by her matter-of-fact presentation of the story. She said, for instance, very reluctantly that the lad was after the maid. From the reluctance it could be

expected that something rather unpleasant was to come, but she continued as follows in an indifferent tone: "The lad was just in love with the girl. This is nothing unusual? This happens often?—oh, now there is something again—no, that I cannot—" etc. While telling the story she always tried from time to time to belittle and talk herself out of her belief in the importance of an event by inserting such generalizing rhetorical questions.

712 From now on, during the whole period of the analysis (three weeks), the original obsessional ideas were absent; their place had been taken by sexual ideas. The memories underlying the obsessional ideas that had already been dealt with constantly tormented the patient. She was so obsessed by these sexual reminiscences that she was never able to find peace until she had told the story again. She expressed great amazement at this change; the stories came like beads on a string, as if they had been experienced yesterday. Things occurred to her of which she had previously been quite unconscious but which she now again recalled (Freud's hypermnesia). Of course, these admissions have to be taken with the same reserve as the familiar "I don't know." The patient may quite well have ardently cultivated all her sexual ideas without remembering them, and spun them out right up to the moment when she had to speak about them objectively. In her stories one can often see immediately what is to come from her gestures, while she still repeatedly asserts that she certainly does not remember anything more. Her everyday person and her sexual person are just two different complexes, two different aspects of consciousness that do not want to or must not know anything of one another. The split of the personality here is, however, only hinted at (as in every vigorous complex, the peculiarity of which is a striving for autonomy). But it is only a step to the classic examples of split personality, all of which are, of course, produced by the mechanisms demonstrated by Freud.[20]

713 With these three sessions a certain conclusion was reached, in so far as one could not avoid relating the obsessional idea that she had caused the death of her former pupil to the self-reproaches connected with the sexual stories. This apparently

20 Cf. Jung, "On the Psychology and Pathology of So-called Occult Phenomena" (1902).

was also felt by the patient when she spontaneously mentioned that many years had already passed since these events, and the thought that she had caused the pupil's death had long ceased to torment her. Probably for the purpose of escaping from the unbearable sexual ideas, she transferred the guilt from this field to that of her educational methods. The mechanism, which is well known, is this: if one has continually to reproach oneself in one sphere, one tries to compensate for these deficiencies in another sphere, as if the same deficiencies were present there as well; this is particularly obvious in masturbators (compulsive brooding, cleanliness, and orderliness). It therefore seems to be not incidental that precisely these stories, underlying a past obsessional idea, were told first. Since there were in present consciousness no obsessional ideas directly supported by these stories, there were no special resistances present. Hence, the stories were relatively immaterial.

714   I refrain from presenting the subsequent sessions in detail; they all followed the pattern already described. No admonition, no pointing out the absurdity of her stereotyped resistance, could make the patient talk more quickly and spontaneously. Every new session was a new torture, and at almost every one the patient declared that this was the last. Usually during the following night, however, there came new material that tormented her.

715   The reminiscences of her time as governess were succeeded by a series of unsavoury stories that had served as a topic for conversation with the neighbour for whose death without the sacraments the patient reproached herself. The neighbour was a person about whose dubious past a number of rumours were current. The patient, who is a very decent girl and comes from a respectable family, known to me, had in her own view a dubious past herself and reproached herself for it. Therefore it is not surprising, psychologically, that she was immediately attracted by the interesting neighbour. There the *chronique scandaleuse* of the day used to be discussed, and in this connection the patient had quite a number of obscene stories and jokes to tell me, which I need not repeat here. For this also she reproached herself. When the neighbour quickly succumbed to an illness, the patient transferred the reproaches, which actually were about her sexual curiosity, to the death of the

neighbour, who had died without absolution because the patient had during her visits enticed her to sinful conversations. The type of reminiscence and of reasoning seems to suggest that this obsessional idea is simply a new version of the earlier obsession about the death of the pupil. The religious obsession took her first to the priest and then to the doctor. She felt that she had infected both of them with her obsessions. She had therefore done something similar to what she had done to the neighbour whom she had destroyed simply by being what she was, as she had originally also destroyed the pupil. Underlying all this is the general idea that she is a horrible creature who infects everything with her depravity.

716   During the following sessions the patient dealt mainly with a series of stories that she had recently discussed with a girl friend. The friend has an office job in a big shop. There she hears quite a number of juicy things from the men, each of which she retails to the patient while they are still warm. On one occasion the friend said she intended to have sexual intercourse just simply to see what it was like. This thought mightily excited the patient; she told herself incessantly that she too would like to have it. This, however, was sufficient reason for renewed self-reproaches. From this incident onwards there was an increasingly clear trend towards referring sexual subjects to herself; during almost every session obscene jokes and the like had to be told again. From the ideas referring to herself there came first all the reminiscences of former love-affairs and longings for affection. The recounting of these on the whole rather harmless events went off fairly smoothly. Only one incident had a stronger emotional charge. She was in love with a young man about whom she knew very little and thought he was going to marry her. Later, however, he left her without a goodbye and she never heard from him again. For a long time she kept on waiting for him and always hoped he would write to her. To this refers 78, *stranger / nostalgia*,[21] 14.8 secs. As already mentioned, the patient could not then explain the significance of this reaction. While the old love stories were told without any major difficulties, once this phase had passed

---

21 [German *fremd/Heimweh*; "fremd" is an adjective the literal translation of which ('strange') would be misleading. The noun had therefore to be used, although not strictly apposite.]

resistance set in. The patient definitely wanted to leave, she had no more to tell. I told her that I had not heard anything about her earlier youth. She thought she would soon be finished with that, there was not much to tell about her youth. She had hardly finished this sentence when she was compelled to repeat several times her vehement tic-like defensive gestures, an unmistakable sign that much more very important material could be expected. With the greatest resistance and the most painful contortions she told in a jerky manner of a book that she had found at home, when she was ten years old, the title of which was *The Way to Happy Matrimony*. She asserted that she had no longer any idea what was in it. But as I continued to be relentless, recollections recurred after a while, and it turned out that the patient still remembered every detail, frequently even the wording. She gave a detailed account of the first sexual intercourse and its complications; the academic description without any personal reference seemed to me peculiar and unusual. I suspected that something must be concealed behind this façade. It was not long before the patient related that at the age of fourteen she had found in her elder brother's pocket a small book in which was reprinted a letter. The letter was written by a young wife to an intimate friend and discussed the secrets of the wedding night in a very obscene and lascivious manner. Apparently I was on the right track, as this story showed. The patient's next recollection concerned erotic dreams that she had had only quite recently. The dreams were outspoken ejaculation dreams and represented sexual intercourse undisguised. This was followed by the confession of having several times tried to hold the dream-image and to masturbate. Then it turned out that masturbation had also occasionally been practised before this. With the masturbation was linked a persistent thinking about her own genitals; she is compelled to wonder whether she "is properly built," whether perhaps she has not a too narrow introitus; she also has to investigate this state of affairs with the finger. She frequently has to look at her naked body in the mirror, etc. She has a long series of fantasies on sexual intercourse, she is compelled especially to imagine in every detail how she would behave during the first intercourse, etc. In this connection she also confesses to feeling a strong libido (which at the beginning she had emphatically denied). She would very much like to get married, and therefore attaches sexual fantasies to most of the men she meets. She also imagines herself in the leading part of all the sex stories she has collected. Thus she tells, for instance, of a naïve young acquaintance, a girl who, on a trip in a crowded railway compartment, had to sit on her teacher's lap. The girl afterwards laughingly related that the teacher never forgot his role, he even carried a ruler in his trousers pocket. About this story the patient thinks that she too would enjoy it if a teacher took her on his lap, but she would know what the ruler in the trousers pocket meant. (The previously not-completely explained reaction [92] *to choose / teacher* may have been constellated partly by this story.)

717   With great reluctance she also admits that at the age of fourteen she had once laid herself upon her younger sister "as if she had been a man." At last, in one of the latest sessions, came the narration of an event which in every respect had the significance of Freud's youth trauma. At the age of seven or eight she had repeatedly listened to the sexual intercourse of her father and mother. Once she noticed that her mother struggled and did not at all want to let the father come to her again. For a long time after that she could not face her parents any more. Then her mother became pregnant and gave birth to her younger sister. She bitterly hated the little sister from the very beginning, and only much later was she able to overcome a deep aversion to the child. It is, of course, not quite unlikely that the patient imagined herself as one of the acting persons in this story and that she adopted the role of the mother. This very plausible connection easily explains the strong emotional charge in all associations to the father.

718   Of course, the psychic trauma of such an observation becomes a complex with a very strong emotional charge in a child's mind, which is bound to constellate the thinking and acting for years to come. This was, in a classic way, the case with this patient. It gave a quite definite direction to her sexual function.[22] This becomes obvious from the analysis of her repressed material; it is always chiefly connected with digging

22 With this one can also compare the fact that many sexually perverted persons (fetishists) have acquired their abnormality through an incidental sexual event (see Krafft-Ebing, *Psychopathia Sexualis*).

out and imagining situations of sexual intercourse. Surprisingly, in spite of her sexually extraordinarily lively fantasy, she never became deeply involved with men and anxiously repulsed every attempt at seduction. But instead she was attracted, with an almost magical force, to doubtful females and dirty topics of conversation which, at her level of education and intelligence, one would not have expected. The two last sessions were particularly instructive in this respect. She produced the choicest selection of most repulsive obscenities that she had occasionally heard in the street. What these obscenities, the narration of which I must be spared, had in common were various abnormalities of sexual intercourse (e.g., too wide, or too narrow introitus, sexual intercourse of a little hunchback with a huge fat woman, etc.). The number and the extreme vulgarity of these jokes appeared to me almost incredible for such an educated and decent lady. The phenomenon, however, is explained by the early perverted direction of the sexual function, which is mainly concerned with finding out unclean sexual practices, i.e., the symbolic repetition of eavesdropping on sexual intercourse. This complex, caused by listening to the sexual act, has throughout her life determined a multitude of sexual actions and associations with their peculiar manifestations. This, for instance, is the reason why the patient performs a sort of sexual intercourse with her little sister, why her listening at the door to hear whether the gardener is coming still haunts her, why she has to carry out the disgusting job of examining her employers' bed, why she has to seek the company of morally dubious people, etc. Her defensive movements and the peculiar pushing forward of the abdomen also show how the effect of the complex spreads in all directions. It is worth noting, too, that she appears at each session in a different dress.

719   Using the sexual function in this way is bound to be incompatible with her otherwise gently disposed character; a rejection and repression of sexuality as absurd as it is repulsive must have taken place, because it is impossible that an educated and sensitive woman can combine these obscenities with the other contents of her mind. These things can only be tolerated when repressed. But they do exist, they actually have a separate ex-

istence, they form a state within the state, they constitute a personality within the personality. Expressed in other words, there are two mental attitudes present, kept apart by strong emotional barriers. The one must not and cannot know anything of the other. This explains the peculiar disturbances of reproduction that counteract the analysis. The ethically superior mind has not the associations of the other at its disposal; she must therefore think she has forgotten these ideas and that she has never known such things. I am therefore inclined to accept that the patient was really convinced that nothing more came into her head, that it was not a lie when she asserted with the greatest persistence that she had no more to say.

720 But even if a complex is still so far repressed, it must yet have a constellating influence on the contents of normal consciousness, for even the deepest split of consciousness does not reach the indivisible basis of the personality. Thus the repression must leave a certain imprint on the conscious processes; the normal consciousness must somehow explain away the emotional condition that a repressed complex leaves behind. What is simpler, therefore, than to produce an idea compatible with normal consciousness as an explanation for the persistently self-reproachful and discontented mood? To explain away the pangs of conscience related to the sins of the governess phase, the patient displaces her self-reproach on to her method of teaching, which she feels must have led to a disastrous result; otherwise she would not persistently experience the feeling of self-reproach when she recalls incidents of that time. As we have already seen, the origin of this obsession acts as a pattern for the obsessional guilt about the neighbour's dying unabsolved. The accumulation of obsessive ideas about the doctor and the priest has its good reason in the fact that these people were not at all indifferent to her sexuality, as the patient admitted to me. By having a sexual effect on her they become in a way accomplices in her wickedness; she therefore expects them to feel equally guilty.

721 After this analysis we can understand the role, still unclear in the associations, that the father plays in her erotic complex. In general the analysis supports to the widest extent the hypotheses suggested by the associations. The associations actually

served as signposts among the maze of ever-changing fantasies that at every stage threatened to put the analyst on the wrong track.

722 The analysis was carried out every other day for three weeks and lasted one and a half to two hours at a time. Although at the end of the three weeks the patient had neither achieved proper sleep nor peace of mind, I discharged her and heard no more of her until the end of November. During the last days of November 1905 she suddenly came to see me and presented herself as cured. After the termination of the treatment she had still been very agitated for about four weeks. Sometimes she was tortured at night by her sexual images, sometimes again by obsessional ideas. In particular the obsession about the neighbour frequently recurred and did not give her any peace until she went to the daughter of the dead woman to make her tell her about the death scene for the nth time. When the daughter told her again, as usual, that the mother had died peacefully, the patient suddenly became convinced that the woman had after all received the last sacraments. With this all obsessional ideas suddenly disappeared. Sleep returned and was only occasionally somewhat disturbed by sexual images.

723 What had brought about this happy ending of the treatment?

724 It is obvious that the daughter's story, which the patient had heard many times without any effect, was nothing but the vehicle for the final removal of the obsession. The actual turn for the better occurred at the beginning of the treatment, when the sexual images replaced the obsessional ideas. The confession of her sinful thoughts may have given considerable relief to the patient. But it seems unlikely that the cure can be ascribed entirely to their verbal expression or to the "abreaction." Pathological ideas can be definitely submerged only by a strong effort. People with obsessions and compulsions are weak; they are unable to keep their ideas in check. Treatment to increase their energy is therefore best for them. The best energy-cure, however, is to force the patients, with a certain ruthlessness, to unearth and expose to the light the images that consciousness finds intolerable. Not only is this a severe challenge for the patient's energy but also his consciousness begins to accept the existence of ideas hitherto repressed.

725 The split-off contents of the mind are destroyed by being released from repression through an effort of the will. So they lose a great deal of their authority and therefore of their horror, and simultaneously the patient regains the feeling of being master of his ideas. I therefore put the emphasis on arousing and strengthening of the will and not on mere "abreacting," as Freud originally did.

726 It appears, from some recent publications, that Freud's theory of obsessional neurosis is still consistently ignored. It therefore gives me great satisfaction to draw attention to Freud's theories—at the risk of also becoming a victim of persistent amnesia.

SUMMARY

727 1. The complex that is brought to light through the associations offered by patients with psychogenic neuroses constitutes the *causa morbi*, apart from any predisposition.

2. The associations may therefore be a valuable aid in finding the pathogenic complex, and may thus be useful for facilitating and shortening Freud's psychoanalysis.

3. The associations supply us with an experimental insight into the psychological foundation of neurotic symptoms: hysteria and obsessive phenomena stem from a complex. The physical and psychic symptoms are nothing but symbolic manifestations of the pathogenic complexes.

FREUD'S THEORY OF HYSTERIA: A REPLY TO ASCHAFFENBURG [1]

1   If I try to answer Aschaffenburg's—on the whole—very moderate and cautious criticism of Freud's theory of hysteria,[2] I do so in order to prevent the baby from being thrown out with the bath-water. Aschaffenburg, of course, does not assert that Freud's importance ends with his theory of hysteria. But the medical public (psychiatrists included) know Freud mainly from this side of his work, and for this reason adverse criticism could easily throw a shadow on Freud's other scientific achievements. I would like to remark at the start that my reply is not directed to Aschaffenburg personally, but to the whole school of thought whose views and aspirations have found eloquent expression in Aschaffenburg's lecture.

2   His criticism is confined exclusively to the role which sexuality, according to Freud, plays in the formation of the psychoneuroses. What he says, therefore, does not affect the wider range of Freud's psychology, that is, the psychology of dreams, jokes, and disturbances of ordinary thinking caused by feeling-toned constellations. It affects only the psychology of sexuality, the determinants of hysterical symptoms, and the methods of psychanalysis.[3] In all these fields Freud has to his credit unique achievements, which can be contested only by one

---

1 [First published as "Die Hysterielehre Freuds: Eine Erwiderung auf die Aschaffenburgsche Kritik," *Münchener medizinische Wochenschrift* (Munich), LIII : 47 (Nov. 1906).—EDITORS.]

2 [Aschaffenburg, "Die Beziehungen des sexuellen Lebens zur Entstehung von Nerven- und Geisteskrankheiten," in the same organ, no. 37 (Sept. 1906). Originally an address (to a congress of neurologists and psychiatrists, Baden-Baden, May 1906) criticizing Freud's "Bruchstück einer Hysterie-analyse," which had been first published in 1905 (i.e., "Fragment of an Analysis of a Case of Hysteria"). See Jones, *Freud: Life and Work*, II, p. 12.—EDITORS.]

3 [The earlier form "psychanalysis" (*Psychanalyse*) is used throughout this and the next paper.—EDITORS.]

33

who has never taken the trouble to check Freud's thought-processes experimentally. I say "achievements," though this does not mean that I subscribe unconditionally to all Freud's theorems. But it is also an achievement, and often no small one, to propound ingenious problems. This achievement cannot be disputed even by Freud's most vigorous opponents.

3   To avoid being unnecessarily diffuse, I shall leave out of account all those points which are not affected by Aschaffenburg's criticism, and shall confine myself only to those it attacks.

4   Freud maintains that he has found the root of *most* psychoneuroses to be a psychosexual trauma. Is this assertion nonsense?

5   Aschaffenburg takes his stand on the view, generally accepted today, that hysteria is a psychogenic illness. It therefore has its roots in the psyche. It would be a work of supererogation to point out that an essential component of the psyche is sexuality, a component of whose extent and importance we can form absolutely no conception in the present unsatisfactory state of empirical psychology. We know only that one meets sexuality everywhere. Is there any other psychic factor, any other basic drive except hunger and its derivates, that has a similar importance in human psychology? I could not name one. It stands to reason that such a large and weighty component of the psyche must give rise to a correspondingly large number of emotional conflicts and affective disturbances, and a glance at real life teaches us nothing to the contrary. Freud's view can therefore claim a high degree of probability at the outset, in so far as he derives hysteria primarily from psychosexual conflicts.

6   Now what about Freud's particular view that all hysteria is reducible to sexuality?

7   Freud has not examined all the hysterias there are. His proposition is therefore subject to the general limitation which applies to empirical axioms. He has simply found his view confirmed in the cases observed by him, which constitute an infinitely small fraction of all cases of hysteria. It is even conceivable that there are several forms of hysteria which Freud has not yet observed at all. Finally, it is also possible that Freud's material, under the constellation of his writings, has become somewhat one-sided.

8   We may therefore modify his dictum, with the consent of the author, as follows: An indefinitely large number of cases of hysteria derive from sexual roots.

9   Has anyone proved that this is not so? By "prove" I naturally
mean applying Freud's psychanalytic methods and not just carrying out a rigorous examination of the patient and then declaring that nothing sexual can be found. All such "proofs" are
of course worthless from the start. Otherwise we would have to
admit that a person who examines a bacterial culture with a
magnifying-glass and asserts that there are no bacteria in it is
right. The application of psychanalytic methods is, logically, a
sine qua non.

10   Aschaffenburg's objection that an entirely traumatic hysteria
contains nothing sexual and goes back to other, very clear traumata seems to me very apt. But the limits of traumatic hysteria,
as Aschaffenburg's example shows (flower-pot falling followed
by aphonia), are very wide. At that rate countless cases of hysteria could be put into the category of "traumatic" hysteria, for
how often does a mild fright produce a new symptom! Aschaffenburg will surely not believe that anyone can be so naïve as to
seek the cause of the symptom in that little affect alone. The
obvious inference is that the patient was hysterical long before.
When for instance a shot is fired and a passing girl gets abasia,
we can safely assume that the vessel, long since full, has merely
overflowed. No special feat of interpretation is needed to prove
this. So these and a legion of similar cases prove nothing against
Freud.

11   It is rather different in the case of physical traumata and
hysterias about insurance money. Here, where the trauma and
the highly affective prospect of money coincide, an emotional
situation arises which makes the outbreak of a specific form of
hysteria appear at least very plausible. It is possible that Freud's
view is not valid in these cases. For lack of other experiences I
incline to this opinion. But if we want to be absolutely fair and
absolutely scientific, we would certainly have to show first that
a sexual constellation really never did pave the way for the hysteria, i.e., that nothing of this sort comes out under analysis. At
any rate the allegation of traumatic hysteria proves, at best,
only that not all cases of hysteria have a sexual root. But this
does not controvert Freud's basic proposition, as modified
above.

12   There is no other way to refute it than by the use of psychanalytic methods. Anyone who does not use them will never
refute Freud; for it must be proved by means of the methods

inaugurated by him that factors can be found in hysteria other than sexual ones, or that these methods are totally unsuited to bringing intimate psychic material to light.

13   Under these conditions, can Aschaffenburg substantiate his criticism?

14   We hear a great deal about "experiments" and "experiences," but there is nothing to show that our critic has used the methods himself and—what is more important—handled them with certainty. He cites a number of—we must admit—very startling examples of Freudian interpretation, which are bound to nonplus the beginner. He himself points out the inadequacy of quotations torn from their context; it should not be too much if I emphasize still further that in psychology the context is everything. These Freudian interpretations are the result of innumerable experiences and inferences. If you present such results naked, stripped of their psychological premises, naturally no one can understand them.

15   When Aschaffenburg says these interpretations are arbitrary and asserts that other interpretations are just as possible, or that there is absolutely nothing behind the facts in question, it is up to him to prove, by his own analyses, that such things are susceptible of altogether different interpretations. Then the matter would be quickly settled, and everyone would thank him for clearing up this question. It is the same with the question of "forgetting" and other symptomatic actions which Aschaffenburg relegates to the realm of mysticism. These phenomena are extraordinarily common; you meet them almost every day. It is therefore not too much to ask a critic to show by means of practical examples how these phenomena can be traced back to other causes. The association experiment would provide him with any amount of material. Again he would be doing constructive work for which one could not thank him enough.

16   As soon as Aschaffenburg meets these requirements, that is to say, publishes psychanalyses with totally different findings, we will accept his criticism, and then the discussion of Freud's theory can be reopened. Till then his criticism hangs in mid air.

17   Aschaffenburg asserts that the psychanalytic method amounts to auto-suggestion on the part of the doctor as well as the patient.

18   Apart from the fact that it is incumbent on a critic to demonstrate his thorough knowledge of the method, we also lack the

proof that the method is auto-suggestion. In earlier writings [4] I have already pointed out that the association experiment devised by me gives the same results in principle, and that psychanalysis is really no different from an association experiment, as Aschaffenburg himself says in his criticism. His assertion that the experiment was used by me in one case only is erroneous; it was used for the purpose of analysis in a great number of cases, as is evident from numerous statements in my own work and from the recent work of Riklin. Aschaffenburg can check my statements and those of Freud at any time, so far as the latter coincide with my own, by experiment, and thereby acquire a knowledge of the exact foundations of psychanalysis.

19   That my experiments have nothing to do with auto-suggestion can easily be seen from their use in the *experimental diagnosis of facts.* The step from the association experiment, which is already pretty complicated, to full psychanalysis is certainly a big one. But, by thorough study of the association experiment —to the development of which Aschaffenburg himself has made outstanding contributions—one can acquire invaluable insights which prove very useful during analysis. (At any rate this has been so with me.) Only when he has gone through this arduous and difficult training can he begin, with some justification, to examine Freud's theory for evidence of auto-suggestion. He will also have a more sympathetic insight into the somewhat apodictic nature of Freud's style. He will learn to understand how uncommonly difficult it is to *describe* these delicate psychological matters. A written exposition will never be able to reproduce the reality of psychanalysis even approximately, let alone reproduce it in such a way that it has an immediately convincing effect on the reader. When I first read Freud's writings it was the same with me as with everybody else: I could only strew the pages with question-marks. And it will be like that for everyone who reads the account of my association

4 *Studies in Word Association.* [Vol. I of *Diagnostische Assoziationsstudien,* which the author actually cited here, was published in 1906, before the present paper. It reprinted Jung's "Psychoanalyse und Assoziationsexperiment" ("Psychoanalysis and Association Experiments," in *Experimental Researches,* Coll. Works, Vol. 2), originally published in the *Journal für Psychologie und Neurologie* (Leipzig), VII (1905). This paper, which discussed Freud's theory of hysteria and commented on the "Fragment of an Analysis" (see n. 2, supra), was Jung's first significant publication on the subject of psychoanalysis.—EDITORS.]

experiments for the first time. Luckily, however, anyone who wants to can repeat them, and so experience for himself what he did not believe before. Unfortunately this is not true of psychanalysis, since it presupposes an unusual combination of specialized knowledge and psychological routine which not everyone possesses, but which can, to a certain extent, be learnt.

20   So long as we do not know whether Aschaffenburg has this practical experience, the charge of auto-suggestion cannot be taken any more seriously than that of arbitrary interpretation.

21   Aschaffenburg regards the exploration of the patient for sexual ideas as, in many cases, immoral.

22   This is a very delicate question, for whenever morals get mixed up with science one can only pit one belief against another belief. If we look at it simply from the utilitarian point of view, we have to ask ourselves whether sexual enlightenment is under all circumstances harmful or not. This question cannot be answered in general terms, because just as many cases can be cited for as against. Everything depends on the individual. Many people can stand certain truths, others not. Every skilled psychologist will surely take account of this fact. Any rigid formula is particularly wrong here. Apart from the fact that there are many patients who are not in the least harmed by sexual enlightenment, there are not a few who, far from having to be pushed towards this theme, guide the analysis to this point of their own accord. Finally, there are cases (of which I have had more than one) that cannot be got at at all until their sexual circumstances are subjected to a thorough review, and in the cases I have known this has led to very good results. It therefore seems to me beyond doubt that there are at least a great many cases where discussion of sexual matters not only does no harm but is positively helpful. Conversely, I do not hesitate to admit that there are cases where sexual enlightenment does more harm than good. It must be left to the skill of the analyst to find out which these cases are. This, it seems to me, disposes of the moral problem. "Higher" moral considerations derive all too easily from some obnoxious schematism, for which reason their application in practice would seem inopportune from the start.

23   So far as the therapeutic effect of psychanalysis is concerned, it makes no difference to the scientific rightness of the hysteria theory or of the analytic method how the therapeutic result

turns out. My personal conviction at present is that Freud's psychanalysis is one of several possible therapies and that in certain cases it achieves more than the others.

24   As to the scientific findings of psychanalysis, nobody should be put off by seeming enormities, and particularly not by sensational quotations. Freud is probably liable to many human errors, but that does not by any means rule out the possibility that a core of truth lies hidden in the crude husk, of whose significance we can form no adequate conception at present. Seldom has a great truth appeared without fantastic wrappings. One has only to think of Kepler and Newton!

25   In conclusion, I would like to utter an urgent warning against the standpoint of Spielmeyer,[5] which cannot be condemned sharply enough. When a person reviles as unscientific not only a theory whose experimental foundations he has not even examined but also those who have taken the trouble to test it for themselves, the freedom of scientific research is imperilled. No matter whether Freud is mistaken or not, he has the right to be heard before the forum of science. Justice demands that Freud's statements should be verified. But to strike them dead and then consign them to oblivion, that is beneath the dignity of an impartial and unprejudiced scientist.

26   To recapitulate:

(1) It has never yet been proved that Freud's theory of hysteria is erroneous in all cases.

(2) This proof can, logically, be supplied only by one who practises the psychanalytic method.

(3) It has not been proved that psychanalysis gives other results than those obtained by Freud.

(4) It has not been proved that psychanalysis is based on false principles and is altogether unsuitable for an understanding of hysterical symptoms.

5 Untitled note in the *Zentralblatt für Nervenheilkunde und Psychiatrie*, XXIX (1906), 322. [The first review (pub. April) of Freud's "Fragment of an Analysis of a Case of Hysteria"; see n. 2, supra. Jung's paper cited in n. 4, supra, is earlier, however, and is probably the first discussion of the "Dora analysis."—EDITORS.]

THE FREUDIAN THEORY OF HYSTERIA [1]

27   It is always a difficult and ungrateful task to discuss a theory which the author himself has not formulated in any final way. Freud has never propounded a cut-and-dried theory of hysteria; he has simply tried, from time to time, to formulate his theoretical conclusions in accordance with his experience at that moment. His theoretical formulations can claim the status of a working hypothesis that agrees with experience at all points. For the present, therefore, there can be no talk of a firmly-established Freudian theory of hysteria, but only of numerous experiences which have certain features in common. As we are not dealing with anything finished and conclusive, but rather with a process of development, an historical survey will probably be the form best suited to an account of Freud's teachings.

28   The theoretical presuppositions on which Freud bases his investigations are to be found in the experiments of Pierre Janet. Breuer and Freud, in their first formulation of the problem of hysteria, start from the fact of psychic dissociation and unconscious psychic automatisms. A further presupposition is the aetiological significance of affects, stressed among others by Binswanger.[2] These two presuppositions, together with the findings reached by the theory of suggestion, culminate in the now generally accepted view that hysteria is a psychogenic neurosis.

29   The aim of Freud's research is to discover how the mechanism producing hysterical symptoms works. Nothing less is attempted, therefore, than to supply the missing link in the long chain between the initial cause and the ultimate symptom, a

---

[1] [Translated from "Die Freud'sche Hysterietheorie," *Monatsschrift für Psychiatrie und Neurologie* (Berlin), XXIII (1908), 310–22. Originally a report to the First International Congress of Psychiatry and Neurology, Amsterdam, September 1907. Aschaffenburg also addressed the Congress, publishing his paper in the same organ, XXII (1907), 564ff. For an account of this event, see Jones, *Freud: Life and Work*, II, pp. 125ff.—EDITORS.]

[2] [L. Binswanger, "Freud'sche Mechanismen in der Symptomatologie von Psychosen" (1906). Cf. Jones, II, pp. 36f.—EDITORS.]

link which no one had yet been able to find. The fact, obvious enough to any attentive observer, that affects play an aetiologically decisive role in the formation of hysterical symptoms makes the findings of the first Breuer-Freud report, in the year 1893, immediately intelligible. This is especially true of the proposition advanced by both authors, that the hysteric suffers most of all from *reminiscences,* i.e., from feeling-toned complexes of ideas which, in certain exceptional conditions, prevent the initial affect from working itself out and finally disappearing.

30   This view, presented only in broad outline at first, was reached by Breuer, who between the years 1880 and 1882 had the opportunity to observe and treat an hysterical woman patient of great intelligence. The clinical picture was characterized chiefly by a profound splitting of consciousness, together with numerous physical symptoms of secondary importance and constancy. Breuer, allowing himself to be guided by the patient, observed that in her twilight states complexes of reminiscences were reproduced which derived from the previous year. In these states she hallucinated a great many episodes that had had a traumatic significance for her. Further, he noticed that the reliving and retelling of these traumatic events had a marked therapeutic effect, bringing relief and an improvement in her condition. If he broke off the treatment, a considerable deterioration set in after a short time. In order to increase and accelerate the effect of the treatment, Breuer induced, besides the spontaneous twilight state, an artificially suggested one in which more material was "abreacted." In this way he succeeded in effecting a substantial improvement. Freud, who at once recognized the extraordinary importance of these observations, thereupon furnished a number of his own which agreed with them. This material can be found in *Studies on Hysteria,* published in 1895 by Breuer and Freud.

31   On this foundation was raised the original theoretical edifice constructed jointly by the two authors. They start with the symptomatology of affects in normal individuals. The excitation produced by affects is converted into a series of somatic innervations, thus exhausting itself and so restoring the "tonus of the nerve centres." In this way the affect is "abreacted." It is different in hysteria. Here the traumatic experience is followed—to use a phrase of Oppenheim's—by an "abnormal expression of

the emotional impulse." [3] The intracerebral excitation is not discharged directly, in a natural way, but produces pathological symptoms, either new ones or a recrudescence of old ones. The excitation is converted into abnormal innervations, a phenomenon which the authors call "conversion of the sum of excitation." The affect is deprived of its normal expression, of its normal outlet in adequate innervations; it is not abreacted but remains "blocked." The resulting hysterical symptoms can therefore be regarded as manifestations of the retention.

32 This formulates the situation as we see it in the patient; but the important question as to why the affect should be blocked and converted still remains unanswered, and it was to this question that Freud devoted special attention. In "The Defence Neuro-psychoses," published in 1894, he tried to analyse in great detail the psychological repercussions of the affect. He found two groups of psychogenic neuroses, different in principle because in one group the pathogenic affect is converted into somatic innervations, while in the other group it is displaced to a different complex of ideas. The first group corresponds to classic hysteria, the second to obsessional neurosis. He found the reason for the blocking of affect, or for its conversion or displacement, to be the incompatibility of the traumatic complex with the normal content of consciousness. In many cases he could furnish direct proof that the incompatibility had reached the consciousness of the patient, thus causing an active repression of the incompatible content. The patient did not wish to know anything about it and treated the critical complex as "non arrivé." The result was a systematic circumvention or "repression" of the vulnerable spot, so that the affect could not be abreacted.

33 The blocking of affect is due, therefore, not to a vaguely conceived "special disposition" but to a recognizable motive.

34 To recapitulate what has been said: up to the year 1895 the Breuer-Freud investigations yielded the following results. Psychogenic symptoms arise from feeling-toned complexes of ideas that have the effect of a trauma, either

    1. by conversion of the excitation into abnormal somatic innervations, or

3 ["Thatsächliches und Hypothetisches über das Wesen der Hysterie" (1890). Cf. Breuer and Freud, *Studies on Hysteria*, Standard Edn., p. 203.—EDITORS.]

2. by displacement of the affect to a less significant complex.

35 The reason why the traumatic affect is not abreacted in a normal way, but is retained, is that its content is not compatible with the rest of the personality and must be repressed.

36 The content of the traumatic affect provided the theme for Freud's further researches. Already in the *Studies on Hysteria* and particularly in "The Defence Neuro-psychoses," Freud had pointed out the sexual nature of the initial affect, whereas the first case history reported by Breuer skirts round the sexual element in a striking fashion, although the whole history not only contains a wealth of sexual allusions but, even for the expert, becomes intelligible and coherent only when the patient's sexuality is taken into account. On the basis of thirteen careful analyses Freud felt justified in asserting that the specific aetiology of hysteria is to be found in the sexual traumata of early childhood, and that the trauma must have consisted in a "real irritation of the genitals." The trauma works at first only preparatorily; it develops its real effect at puberty, when the old memory-trace is reactivated by nascent sexual feelings. Thus Freud tried to resolve the vague concept of a special disposition into quite definite, concrete events in the pre-pubertal period. At that time he did not attribute much significance to a still earlier *inborn* disposition.

37 While the Breuer-Freud *Studies* enjoyed a certain amount of recognition (although, despite Raimann's assurances,[4] they have not yet become the common property of science), *this* theory of Freud's met with general opposition. Not that the frequency of sexual traumata in childhood could be doubted, but rather their exclusively pathogenic significance for normal children. Freud certainly did not evolve this view out of nothing, he was merely formulating certain experiences which had forced themselves on him during analysis. To begin with, he found memory-traces of sexual scenes in infancy, which in many cases were quite definitely related to real happenings. Further, he found that though the traumata remained without specific effect in childhood, after puberty they proved to be determinants of hysterical symptoms. Freud therefore felt compelled to grant that the trauma was real. In my personal opinion he

4 [Emil Raimann, Vienna psychiatrist, critic of Freud. See Jones, I, pp. 395f., and II, p. 122.—EDITORS.]

did this because at that time he was still under the spell of the original view that the hysteric "suffers from reminiscences," for which reason the cause and motivation of the symptom must be sought in the past. Obviously such a view of the aetiological factors was bound to provoke opposition, especially among those with experience of hysteria, for the practitioner is accustomed to look for the driving forces of hysterical neurosis not so much in the past as in the present.

38 This formulation of the theoretical standpoint in 1896 was no more than a transitional stage for Freud, which he has since abandoned. The discovery of sexual determinants in hysteria became the starting-point for extensive researches in the field of sexual psychology in general. Similarly, the problem of the determination of associative processes led his inquiry into the field of dream psychology. In 1900 he published his fundamental work on dreams, which is of such vital importance for the development of his views and his technique. No one who is not thoroughly acquainted with Freud's method of dream interpretation will be able to understand the conceptions he has developed in recent years. *The Interpretation of Dreams* lays down the principles of Freudian theory and at the same time its technique. For an understanding of his present views and the verification of his results a knowledge of Freud's technique is indispensable. This fact makes it necessary for me to go rather more closely into the nature of psychanalysis.

39 The original cathartic method started with the symptoms and sought to discover the traumatic affect underlying them. The affect was thus raised to consciousness and abreacted in the normal manner; that is, it was divested of its traumatic potency. The method relied to a certain extent on suggestion—the analyst took the lead, while the patient remained essentially passive. Aside from this inconvenience, however, it was found that there were more and more cases in which no real trauma was present, and in which all the emotional conflicts seemed to derive exclusively from morbid fantasy activity. The cathartic method was unable to do justice to these cases.

40 According to Freud's statements in 1904,[5] much has altered

5 ["Freud's Psycho-Analytic Procedure" and "On Psychotherapy" appear to be the publications Jung referred to. Cf., however, "Fragment of an Analysis of a Case of Hysteria" (1905), Standard Edn., p. 12.—EDITORS.]

in the method since those early days. All suggestion is now discarded. The patients are no longer guided by the analyst; the freest rein is given to their associations, so that it is really the patients who conduct the analysis. Freud contents himself with registering, and from time to time pointing out, the connections that result. If an interpretation is wrong, it cannot be forced on the patient; if it is right, the result is immediately visible and expresses itself very clearly in the patient's whole behaviour.

41   The present psychanalytic method of Freud is much more complicated, and penetrates much more deeply, than the original cathartic method. Its aim is to bring to consciousness all the false associative connections produced by the complex, and in that way to resolve them. Thus the patient gradually gains complete insight into his illness, and also has an objective standpoint from which to view his complexes. The method could be called an educative one, since it changes the whole thinking and feeling of the patient in such a way that his personality gradually breaks free from the compulsion of the complexes and can take up an independent attitude towards them. In this respect Freud's new method bears some resemblance to the educative method of Dubois,[6] the undeniable success of which is due mainly to the fact that the instruction it imparts alters the patient's attitude towards his complexes.

42   Since it has grown entirely out of empirical practice, the theoretical foundations of the psychanalytic method are still very obscure. By means of my association experiments I think I have made at least a few points accessible to experimental investigation, though not all the theoretical difficulties have been overcome. It seems to me that the main difficulty is this. If, as psychanalysis presupposes, free association leads to the complex, Freud logically assumes that this complex is associated with the starting-point or initial idea. Against this it can be argued that it is not very difficult to establish the associative connection between a cucumber and an elephant. But that is to forget, first, that in analysis only the starting-point is given, and not the goal; and second, that the conscious state is not one of directed thinking but of relaxed attention. Here one might object that the *complex* is the point being aimed at and that, because of its

6 [Paul Dubois, of Bern, treated neurosis by "persuasion."—Editors.]

independent feeling-tone, it possesses a strong tendency to reproduction, so that it "rises up" spontaneously and then, as though purely by chance, appears associated with the starting-point.

43   This is certainly conceivable in theory, but in practice things generally look different. The complex, in fact, does not "rise up" freely but is blocked by the most intense resistances. Instead, what "rises up" often seems at first sight to be quite incomprehensible intermediate associations, which neither the analyst nor the patient recognizes as belonging in any way to the complex. But once the chain leading to the complex has been fully established, the meaning of each single link becomes clear, often in the most startling way, so that no special work of interpretation is needed. Anyone with enough practical experience of analysis can convince himself over and over again that under these conditions not just *anything* is reproduced, but always something that is related to the complex, though the relationship is, *a priori*, not always clear. One must accustom oneself to the thought that even in these chains of association chance is absolutely excluded. So if an associative connection is discovered in a chain of associations which was not intended—if, that is to say, the complex we find is associatively connected with the initial idea—then this connection has existed from the start; in other words, the idea we took as the starting-point was already constellated by the complex. We are therefore justified in regarding the initial idea as a sign or symbol of the complex.

44   This view is in agreement with already known psychological theories which maintain that the psychological situation at a given moment is nothing but the resultant of all the psychological events preceding it. Of these the most predominant are the affective experiences, that is, the complexes, which for that reason have the greatest constellating power. If you take any segment of the psychological present, it will logically contain all the antecedent individual events, the affective experiences occupying the foreground, according to the degree of their actuality. This is true of every particle of the psyche. Hence it is theoretically possible to reconstruct the constellations from every particle, and that is what the Freudian method tries to do. During this work the probability is that you will come upon just the

affective constellation lying closest to hand, and not merely on one but on many, indeed very many, each according to the degree of its constellating power. Freud has called this fact *over-determination.*

45   Psychanalysis accordingly keeps within the bounds of known psychological facts. The method is extraordinarily difficult to apply, but it can be learnt; only, as Löwenfeld rightly emphasizes, one needs some years of intensive practice before one can handle it with any certainty. For this reason alone all over-hasty criticism of Freud's findings is precluded. It also precludes the method from ever being used for mass therapy in mental institutions. Its achievements as a scientific instrument can be judged only by one who uses it himself.

46   Freud applied his method first of all to the investigation of dreams, refining and perfecting it in the process. Here he found, it appears, all those surprising associative connections which play such an important role in the neuroses. I would mention, as the most important discovery, the significant role which feeling-toned complexes play in dreams and their symbolical mode of expression. Freud attaches great significance to verbal expression—one of the most important components of our thinking—because the double meaning of words is a favourite channel for the displacement and improper expression of affects. I mention this point because it is of fundamental importance in the psychology of neurosis. For anyone who is familiar with these matters, which are everyday occurrences with normal people too, the interpretations given in the "Fragment of an Analysis of a Case of Hysteria," however strange they may sound, will contain nothing unexpected, but will fit smoothly into his general experience. Unfortunately I must refrain from a detailed discussion of Freud's findings and must limit myself to a few hints. These latest investigations are required reading for Freud's present view of hysterical illnesses. Judging by my own experience, it is impossible to understand the meaning of the *Three Essays* and of the "Fragment" without a thorough knowledge of *The Interpretation of Dreams.*

47   By "thorough knowledge" I naturally do not mean the cheap philological criticism which many writers have levelled at this book, but a patient application of Freud's principles to psychic processes. Here lies the crux of the whole problem. Attack and

47

defence both miss the mark so long as the discussion proceeds only on theoretical ground. Freud's discoveries do not, at present, lend themselves to the framing of general theories. For the present the only question is: do the associative connections asserted by Freud exist or not? Nothing is achieved by thoughtless affirmation or negation; one should look at the facts without prejudice, carefully observing the rules laid down by Freud. Nor should one be put off by the obtrusion of sexuality, for as a rule you come upon many other, exceedingly interesting things which, at least to begin with, show no trace of sex. An altogether harmless but most instructive exercise, for instance, is the analysis of constellations indicating a complex in the association experiment. With the help of this perfectly harmless material a great many Freudian phenomena can be studied without undue difficulty. The analysis of dreams and hysteria is considerably more difficult and therefore less suitable for a beginner. Without a knowledge of the ground-work Freud's more recent teachings are completely incomprehensible, and, as might be expected, they have remained misunderstood.

48   It is with the greatest hesitation, therefore, that I make the attempt to say something about the subsequent development of Freud's views. My task is rendered especially difficult by the fact that actually we have only two publications to go on: they are the above-mentioned *Three Essays on the Theory of Sexuality* and the "Fragment of an Analysis of a Case of Hysteria." There is as yet no attempt at a systematic exposition and documentation of Freud's more recent views. Let us first try to come closer to the argument of the *Three Essays*.

49   These essays are extremely difficult to understand, not only for one unaccustomed to Freud's way of thinking but also for those who have already worked in this special field. The first thing to be considered is that Freud's conception of sexuality is uncommonly wide. It includes not only normal sexuality but all the perversions, and extends far into the sphere of psychosexual derivates. When Freud speaks of sexuality, it must not be understood merely as the sexual instinct.[7] Another concept which Freud uses in a very wide sense is "libido." This concept, originally borrowed from "libido sexualis," denotes in the first

[7] Freud's concept of sexuality includes roughly everything covered by the concept of the instinct for the preservation of the species.

place the sexual components of psychic life so far as they are volitional, and then any inordinate passion or desire.

50 Infantile sexuality, as Freud understands it, is a bundle of possibilities for the application or "investment" of libido. A normal sexual goal does not exist at that stage, because the sexual organs are not yet fully developed. But the psychic mechanisms are probably already in being. The libido is distributed among all the possible forms of sexual activity, and also among all the perversions—that is, among all the variants of sexuality which, if they become fixed, later turn into real perversions. The progressive development of the child gradually eliminates the libidinal investment of perverse tendencies and concentrates on the growth of normal sexuality. The investments set free during this process are used as driving-forces for sublimations, that is, for the higher mental functions. At or after puberty the normal individual seizes on an objective sexual goal, and with this his sexual development comes to an end.

51 In Freud's view, it is characteristic of hysteria that the infantile sexual development takes place under difficult conditions, since the perverse investments of libido are much less easily discarded than with normal individuals and therefore last longer. If the real sexual demands of later life impinge in any form on a morbid personality, its inhibited development shows itself in the fact that it is unable to satisfy the demand in the proper way, because the demand comes up against an unprepared sexuality. As Freud says, the individual predisposed to hysteria brings a "bit of sexual repression" with him from his childhood. Instead of the sexual excitation, in the widest sense of the word, being acted out in the sphere of normal sexuality, it is repressed and causes a reactivation of the original infantile sexual activity. This is expressed above all in the fantasy-activity so characteristic of hysterics. The fantasies develop along the line already traced by the special kind of infantile sexual activity. The fantasies of hysterics are, as we know, boundless; hence, if the psychic balance is in some measure to be preserved, equivalent inhibiting mechanisms are needed or, as Freud calls them, resistances. If the fantasies are of a sexual nature, then the corresponding resistances will be shame and disgust. As these affective states are normally associated with physical manifestations, the appearance of physical symptoms is assured.

52   I think a concrete example from my own experience will illustrate the meaning of Freud's teachings better than any theoretical formulations, which, because of the complexity of the subject, are all apt to sound uncommonly ponderous.

53   The case is one of psychotic hysteria in an intelligent young woman of twenty. The earliest symptoms occurred between the third and fourth year. At that time the patient began to keep back her stool until pain compelled her to defecate. Gradually she began to employ the following auxiliary procedure: she seated herself in a crouching position on the heel of one foot, and in this position tried to defecate, pressing the heel against the anus. The patient continued this perverse activity until her seventh year. Freud calls this infantile perversion anal eroticism.

54   The perversion stopped with the seventh year and was replaced by masturbation. Once, when her father smacked her on the bare buttocks, she felt distinct sexual excitement. Later she became sexually excited when she saw her younger brother being disciplined in the same way. Gradually she developed a markedly negative attitude towards her father.

55   Puberty started when she was thirteen. From then on fantasies developed of a thoroughly perverse nature which pursued her obsessively. These fantasies had a compulsive character: she could never sit at table without thinking of defecation while she was eating, nor could she watch anyone else eating without thinking of the same thing, and especially not her father. In particular, she could not see her father's hands without feeling sexual excitement; for the same reason she could no longer bear to touch his right hand. Thus it gradually came about that she could not eat at all in the presence of other people without continual fits of compulsive laughter and cries of disgust, because the defecation fantasies finally spread to all the persons in her environment. If she was corrected or even reproached in any way, she answered by sticking out her tongue, or with convulsive laughter, cries of disgust, and gestures of horror, because each time she had before her the vivid image of her father's chastising hand, coupled with sexual excitement, which immediately passed over into ill-concealed masturbation.

56   At the age of fifteen, she felt the normal urge to form a love relationship with another person. But all attempts in this direction failed, because the morbid fantasies invariably thrust

themselves between her and the very person she most wanted to love. At the same time, because of the disgust she felt, any display of affection for her father had become impossible. Her father had been the object of her infantile libido transference, hence the resistances were directed especially against him, whereas her mother was not affected by them. About this time she felt a stirring of love for her teacher, but it quickly succumbed to the same overpowering disgust. In a child so much in need of affection this emotional isolation was bound to have the gravest consequences, which were not long in coming.

57 At eighteen, her condition had got so bad that she really did nothing else than alternate between deep depressions and fits of laughing, crying, and screaming. She could no longer look anyone in the face, kept her head bowed, and when anybody touched her stuck her tongue out with every sign of loathing.

58 This short history demonstrates the essentials of Freud's view. First we find a fragment of perverse infantile sexual activity—anal eroticism—replaced in the seventh year by masturbation. At this period the administering of corporal punishment, affecting the region of the anus, produced sexual excitement. Here we have the determinants for the later psychosexual development. Puberty, with its physical and spiritual upheavals, brought a marked increase in fantasy activity. This seized on the sexual activity of childhood and modulated it in endless variations. Perverse fantasies of this kind were bound to act as moral foreign bodies, so to speak, in an otherwise sensitive person, and had to be repressed by means of defence mechanisms, particularly shame and disgust. This readily accounts for all those fits of disgust, loathing, exclamations of horror, sticking out the tongue, etc.

59 At the time when the ordinary longings of puberty for the love of other people were beginning to stir, the pathological symptoms increased, because the fantasies were now directed most intensively to the very people who seemed most worthy of love. This naturally led to a violent psychic conflict, which fully explains the deterioration that then set in, ending in hysterical psychosis.

60 We now understand why Freud can say that hysterics bring with them "a bit of sexual repression from childhood." For constitutional reasons they are probably ready for sexual or quasi-

51

sexual activities earlier than other people. In keeping with their constitutional emotivity, the infantile impressions go deeper and last longer, so that later, at puberty, they have a constellating effect on the trend of the first really sexual fantasies. Again in keeping with their constitutional emotivity, all affective impulses are much stronger than in normal persons. Hence, to counteract the intensity of their abnormal fantasies, correspondingly strong feelings of shame and disgust are bound to appear. When real sexual demands are made, requiring the transference of libido to the love-object, all the perverse fantasies are transferred to him, as we have seen. Hence the resistance against the object of love. The patient could not transfer her libido to him without inhibitions, and this precipitated the great emotional conflict. Her libido exhausted itself in struggling against her feelings of defence, which grew ever stronger, and which then produced the symptoms. Thus Freud can say that the symptoms represent nothing but the sexual activity of the patient.

61   Summing up, we can formulate Freud's present view of hysteria as follows:

a. Certain precocious sexual activities of a more or less perverse nature grow up on a constitutional basis.

b. These activities do not lead at first to real hysterical symptoms.

c. At puberty (which psychologically sets in earlier than physical maturity) the fantasies tend in a direction constellated by the infantile sexual activity.

d. The fantasies, intensified for constitutional (affective) reasons, lead to the formation of complexes of ideas that are incompatible with the other contents of consciousness and are therefore repressed, chiefly by shame and disgust.

e. This repression takes with it the transference of libido to a love-object, thus precipitating the great emotional conflict which then provides occasion for the outbreak of actual illness.

f. The symptoms of the illness owe their origin to the struggle of the libido against the repression; they therefore represent nothing but an abnormal sexual activity.

62   How far does the validity of Freud's view go? This question is exceedingly difficult to answer. Above all, it must be emphatically pointed out that cases which conform exactly to Freud's schema really do exist. Anyone who has learnt the technique

knows this. But no one knows whether Freud's schema is applicable to all forms of hysteria (in any case, hysteria in children and the psychotraumatic neuroses form a group apart). For ordinary cases of hysteria, such as the nerve-specialist meets by the dozen, Freud asserts the validity of his views; my own experience, which is considerably less than his, has yielded nothing that would argue against this assertion. In the cases of hysteria which I have analysed, the symptoms were extraordinarily varied, but they all showed a surprising similarity in their psychological structure. The outward appearance of a case loses much of its interest when it is analysed, because one then sees how the same complex can produce apparently very far-fetched and very remarkable symptoms. For this reason it is impossible to say whether Freud's schema applies only to certain groups of symptoms. At present we can only affirm that his findings are true of an indefinitely large number of cases of hysteria which till now could not be delimited as clinical groups.

63   As to the detailed results of Freud's analyses, the violent opposition they have met with is due simply to the fact that practically no one has followed the development of Freud's theory since 1896. Had his dream-analyses been tested and his rules observed, Freud's latest publications, particularly the "Fragment of an Analysis of a Case of Hysteria," would not have been so difficult to understand. The only disconcerting thing about these reports is their frankness. The public can forgive Freud least of all for his sexual symbolism. In my view he is really easiest to follow here, because this is just where mythology, expressing the fantasy-thinking of all races, has prepared the ground in the most instructive way. I would only mention the writings of Steinthal [8] in the 1860's, which prove the existence of a widespread sexual symbolism in the mythological records and the history of language. I also recall the eroticism of our poets and their allegorical or symbolical expressions. No one who considers this material will be able to conceal from himself that there are uncommonly far-reaching and significant analogies between the Freudian symbolisms and the symbols of poetic fantasy in individuals and in whole nations. The Freudian symbol and its interpretation is therefore nothing unheard of, it is

8 [Heymann Steinthal (1823–99), German philologist and philosopher. Cf. *Symbols of Transformation,* index, s.v.—EDITORS.]

merely something unusual for us psychiatrists. But these difficulties should not deter us from going more deeply into the
problems raised by Freud, for they are of extraordinary importance for psychiatry no less than for neurology.

A CONTRIBUTION TO THE PSYCHOLOGY
OF RUMOUR [1]

95   About a year ago the school authorities in N. asked me to
furnish a report on the mental condition of Marie X., a thir-
teen-year-old school-girl. Marie had recently been expelled from
the school because she was instrumental in originating an ugly
rumour, spreading gossip about her class-teacher. The punishment hit the child, and especially her parents, very hard, so
that the school authorities were inclined to readmit her under
the cover of a medical opinion.

96   The facts of the case were as follows. The teacher had heard
indirectly that the girls were telling an ambiguous sexual story
about him. On investigation, it was found that Marie had one
day related a dream to three girl-friends which ran somewhat
as follows:

*The class was going to the bathing-place. I had to go with
the boys because there was no more room.—Then we swam a
long way out in the lake.* (Asked "Who?" Marie said: "Lina,[2]
the teacher, and me.") *A steamer came along. The teacher asked
us: "Do you want a ride?" We came to K. A wedding was going
on.* ("Whose?" "A friend of the teacher's.") *We were allowed to
take part in it. Then we went on a journey.* ("Who?" "Me, Lina,
and the teacher.") *It was like a honeymoon trip. We came to
Andermatt, and there was no more room in the hotel so we had
to spend the night in a barn. There the woman got a child and
the teacher became the godfather.*

97   This dream was told me by the child when I examined her.
The teacher had also got her to tell the dream in writing. In this
earlier version the obvious gap after "Do you want a ride?" was

1 [Originally published as "Ein Beitrag zur Psychologie des Gerüchtes," *Zentralblatt für Psychoanalyse* (Wiesbaden), I (1910/11): 3, 81–90. Previously translated
in *Collected Papers on Analytical Psychology* (London and New York, 1916;
2nd edn., 1917).—EDITORS.]
2 [Her sister. Cf. par. 119.—EDITORS.]

filled in by the words: "We got on it. Soon we felt cold. An old man gave us a blouse which the teacher put on." On the other hand, there was an omission of the passage about finding no room in the hotel and having to spend the night in the barn.

98   The child told the dream immediately not only to her three friends but also to her mother. The mother repeated it to me with only trifling differences from the two readings given above. In his investigations, carried out with the deepest misgivings, the teacher failed, like myself, to discover any other, more dangerous text. It is therefore very probable that the original story could not have been very different. (The passage about the cold and the blouse seems to be an early interpolation, as it tries to establish a logical relationship. Coming out of the water one is wet, has on only a bathing-dress, and therefore cannot take part in a wedding before putting on some clothes.) The teacher would not believe at first that it was simply a dream, he suspected it was an invention. But he had to admit that the innocent telling of the dream was apparently a fact, and that it would be unnatural to credit the child with sufficient guile to make sexual innuendoes in such a veiled form. For a time he wavered between the view that it was a cunning invention and the view that it was really a dream, harmless in itself, which had been given a sexual twist by the other children. When his first indignation wore off he came to see that Marie's guilt could not be so great, and that the fantasies of her friends had contributed to the rumour. He then did something very praiseworthy: he placed Marie's schoolmates under supervision and made them all write out what they had heard of the dream.

99   Before turning our attention to these accounts, let us first consider the dream analytically. To begin with, we must accept the facts and agree with the teacher that it really was a dream and not an invention—the ambiguities are too great for that. Conscious invention tries to create unbroken transitions; the dream takes no account of this, but proceeds regardless of gaps, which, as we have seen, give rise to interpolations during the conscious revision. The gaps are very significant. In the bathing-place there is no picture of undressing, being unclothed, nor any detailed description of being together in the water. The lack of clothes on the steamer is compensated by the above-mentioned interpolation, but only for the teacher, which shows

that his nakedness was most urgently in need of cover. There is no detailed description of the wedding, and the transition from the steamer to the wedding celebration is abrupt. The reason for stopping overnight in the barn at Andermatt is undiscoverable at first. The parallel, however, is the lack of room in the bathing-place, which made it necessary for the girls to go to the men's section; the lack of room at the hotel again prevents the segregation of the sexes. The picture of the barn is very inadequately filled out: the birth follows suddenly and disconnectedly. The teacher as godfather is extremely ambiguous. Marie's role throughout the whole story is of secondary importance; she is no more than a spectator.

100   All this has the appearance of a genuine dream, and those of my readers who have sufficient experience of dreams of girls of this age will certainly confirm this view. The interpretation of the dream is so simple that we can safely leave it to the children themselves, whose statements now follow.

Aural Witnesses

101   (1) Marie dreamt that she and Lina went swimming with our teacher. When they had swum out pretty far in the lake, Marie said she could not swim any further, her foot hurt her so. Our teacher said, she could ride on my back. Marie got on and they swam out together. After a while a steamer came along and they got on it. It seems our teacher had a rope with him with which he tied Marie and Lina together, and so pulled them out into the lake after him. They went as far as Z., where they got out. But now they had no clothes on. The teacher bought a jacket, and Marie and Lina got a long thick veil, and all three walked up the street by the lake. This was when the wedding was going on. Soon they met. The bride had on a blue silk dress but no veil. She asked Marie and Lina if they would be so kind as to give her their veil. Marie and Lina gave it and in return were allowed to go to the wedding. They went to the Sun Inn. Afterwards they made a honeymoon trip to Andermatt, I don't know whether they went to the inn at Andermatt or at Z. There they were given coffee, potatoes, honey, and butter. I must not say any more, only that in the end the teacher became the god-father.

102   Here the roundabout story of lack of room at the bathing-place is missing; Marie goes swimming with the teacher right

away. Their being together in the water is given a more personal relationship by the rope connecting the teacher and the two girls. The ambiguity about the "ride" [3] in the original story has already had consequences here, for the part about the steamer now takes second place, and first place is given to the teacher, who takes Marie on his back. (The delightful little slip "she could ride on my back"—instead of *his*—shows the narrator's inner participation in the scene.) This explains why she brings the steamer into action somewhat abruptly, in order to give the equivocal "ride" a familiar, harmless turn, like the anticlimax in a music-hall song. The passage about the lack of clothes, the ambiguity of which has already been noted, arouses her special interest. The teacher buys a jacket, the girls get a long thick veil, such as is worn only in case of death or at weddings. That the wedding is meant here in a wider sense is shown by the remark that the bride had no veil: the one who has the veil is the bride! The narrator, a good friend of Marie, helps her to dream the dream further: the possession of the veil characterizes Marie and Lina as brides. Anything offensive or immoral in this situation is relieved by the girls' surrendering the veil; the narrator thus gives the story an innocent turn. The same mechanism is followed in the embellishment of the ambiguous situation at Andermatt: there is nothing but nice things, coffee, potatoes, honey, and butter, a reversion to the infantile on the well-known pattern. The conclusion seems to be very abrupt: the teacher becomes a godfather.

103   (2) Marie dreamt that she went bathing with Lina and the teacher. Far out in the lake Marie told the teacher her leg was hurting. The teacher said she could ride on his back. I don't know now whether the last sentence was really told so, but I think it was. As there was a ship on the lake just then, the teacher said she should swim to the ship and then get in. I really don't remember any more how she told it.—Then the teacher or Marie, I don't know which, said they would get out at Z. and run home. So the teacher called to two gentlemen, who had just been bathing, to carry the children ashore. Lina sat on one man's back and Marie on the other fat man,

---

3 [*Aufsitzen* in the original. The word (usually intransitive) means both to 'sit on a person's back' and to 'mount' a horse or vehicle. As applied to a steamer, its use is quite exceptional. The ambiguity can be preserved in English only by alternating between 'ride' and 'get on.'—TRANS.]

and the teacher held on to the fat man's leg and swam after them. When they landed they ran home.

On the way the teacher met his friend, who had a wedding. Marie said, it was then the fashion to go on foot, not in a carriage. Then the bride said they could come along too. Then the teacher said it would be nice if the two girls gave the bride their black veil, which they had got on the way, I don't know where. The girls gave it to her, and the bride said they were nice generous children. Then they went on further and stopped at the Sun Inn. There they had something to eat, I don't know what. Then they went on the honeymoon trip to Andermatt. They went into a barn and danced. All the men had taken off their coats except the teacher. The bride said he should take off his coat too. The teacher refused, but at last he did. Then the teacher was . . . The teacher said he felt cold. I mustn't tell any more, it is improper. That's all I heard of the dream.

104   The narrator pays special attention to the "ride," but is uncertain whether in the original story it referred to the teacher or the steamer. This uncertainty is amply compensated by the elaborate story of the two strange gentlemen who took the girls on their backs. For her, the piggyback is too valuable a thought to be relinquished, only she is embarrassed at the idea of the teacher as its object. The lack of clothes likewise arouses strong interest. The bridal veil has now become black, like a veil of mourning (naturally in order to conceal anything indelicate). Here the innocent turn has even been given a virtuous accent ("nice generous children"); the immoral wish has surreptitiously changed into something virtuous on which special emphasis is laid, suspect like every accentuated virtue. The narrator has exuberantly filled in the blanks in the scene of the barn; the men take off their coats, the teacher follows suit and is consequently . . . naked, and feels cold. Whereupon it becomes too "improper." She has correctly recognized the parallels we conjectured above when discussing the original story, and has added the undressing scene—which really belongs to the bathing scene—here, for it had to come out in the end that the girls were together with the naked teacher.

105   (3) Marie told me she had dreamt: Once I went bathing but there was no more room. The teacher took me into his cabin. I undressed and went bathing. I swam until I reached the bank. There I met the teacher. He said, wouldn't I like to swim across the lake

with him? I went, and Lina also. We swam out and were soon in the middle of the lake. I did not want to swim any further. Now I can't remember it exactly. Soon a ship came along and we got on the ship. The teacher said, "I'm cold," and a sailor gave us an old shirt. Each of us tore a piece off. I tied it round my neck. Then we left the ship and swam on to K.

Lina and I did not want to go any further and two fat men took us on their backs. In K. we got a veil which we put on. In K. we went into the street. The teacher met his friend who invited us to his wedding. We went to the Sun Inn and played games. We also danced the polonaise. Now I don't remember exactly. Afterwards we went on the honeymoon trip to Andermatt. The teacher had no money with him and stole some chestnuts. The teacher told us, "I am so glad I can travel with my two pupils." Now comes something improper which I will not write. Now the dream is finished.

106   Here the undressing together takes place in the bathing-cabin. The lack of clothes on the ship gives rise to a new variant (old shirt torn into three pieces). Because of its uncertainty, the sitting on the teacher is not mentioned. Instead, the girls sit on the backs of two fat men. As "fat" is stressed in this and the previous version, it is worth mentioning that the teacher was more than a little plump. The substitution is typical: each of the girls has a teacher. Duplication or multiplication of personalities expresses their significance, i.e., their investment with libido. The same is true of the repetition of actions.[4] The significance of this multiplication is especially clear in religion and mythology. (Cf. the Trinity and the two mystic formulae of confession: "Isis una quae es omnia," "Hermes omnia solus et ter unus.") Proverbially we say: "He eats, drinks, or sleeps 'for two.' " Also, the multiplication of personality expresses an analogy or comparison: *my friend* has the "same aetiological value" as *myself* (Freud). In dementia praecox, or schizophrenia, to use Bleuler's broader and better term, the multiplication of personality is primarily the expression of libido investment, for it is invariably the person to whom the patient has a transference who is liable to multiplication. ("There are two Professor N.'s." "Oh, so you are Dr. Jung too. This morning another person came to see me who also called himself Dr. Jung.") It seems

4 Cf. the duplication of attributes in dementia praecox in my "The Psychology of Dementia Praecox."

that, in keeping with the general tendency of schizophrenia, this splitting is an analytical depotentiation for the purpose of preventing too powerful impressions. A further significance of the multiplication of personality, though it does not come exactly into this category, is the raising of some attribute to a living figure. A simple example is Dionysus and his companion Phales, Phales (*phallos*) being the personification of the penis of Dionysus. The so-called Dionysian train (satyrs, tityrs, Sileni, maenads, Mimallones, etc.) consists of personifications of Dionysian attributes.

107   The scene in Andermatt is portrayed with a nice wit, or more correctly, is dreamt further. "The teacher stole some chestnuts" is equivalent to saying that he did something prohibited. By chestnuts is meant roast chestnuts, which because of the split are known to be female sexual symbols. Hence the teacher's remark that he was "so glad to travel with his two pupils," following directly on the theft of the chestnuts, becomes understandable. The theft of the chestnuts is certainly a personal interpolation, for it occurs in no other account. It shows how intense was the inner participation of her schoolmates in Marie's dream, i.e., it had the "same aetiological value" for them.

108   This is the last of the aural witnesses. The story of the veil and the pain in the foot or leg are items which may well have been mentioned in the original narrative. Other interpolations are altogether personal and are based on inner participation in the meaning of the dream.

Hearsay Evidence

109   (1) The whole school went bathing with the teacher. Only Marie had no room to undress in the bathing-place. So the teacher said, "You can come into my room and undress with me." She must have felt very uncomfortable. When both were undressed they went into the lake. The teacher took a long cord and tied it round Marie. Then they both swam far out. But Marie got tired, so the teacher took her on his back. Then Marie saw Lina, she called out, "Come with me," and Lina came. They all swam out still further. They met a ship. Then the teacher asked, "May we get in? These girls are tired." The ship stopped and they all got in. I don't know exactly how they came ashore at K. Then the teacher got an old night-shirt. He put it on. Then he met a friend who was having a wedding.

Teacher, Marie, and Lina were invited. The wedding was celebrated at the Crown in K. They wanted to dance the polonaise. The teacher said he would not do it. But the others said he might as well. He did it with Marie. Teacher said, "I will not go home any more to my wife and children. I love you best, Marie." She was very pleased. After the wedding there was a honeymoon trip. Teacher, Marie, and Lina were allowed to go with them. The trip was to Milan. Afterwards they went to Andermatt, where they could find no place to sleep. They went to a barn, where they could stop the night all together. I must not tell any more because it becomes very indecent.

110   The undressing scene at the bathing-place is fully developed. The swim undergoes a simplification for which the story of the rope had paved the way: the teacher ties himself to Marie, but Lina is not mentioned here, she comes only later when Marie was already sitting on the teacher's back. Here the clothing is a night-shirt. The wedding celebrations are given a very direct interpretation: the teacher does not want to go home any more to his wife and children, he loves Marie best. In the barn they found a place "all together" and then it "became very indecent."

111   (2) They said she had gone with the school to the bathing-place to bathe. But as the bathing-place was too full, the teacher called her to come with him. Then we swam out in the lake and Lina followed us. Then the teacher took a cord and tied us together. I don't know exactly how they got separated again. But after a long time they suddenly arrived at Z. There a scene is said to have taken place which I would rather not tell, for if it was true it would be too shameful. Also I don't know exactly what is supposed to have happened as I was very tired. Only I have heard that Marie said she was always to remain with the teacher now, and that he hugged her again and again as his best pupil. If I knew exactly I would also tell the other thing, but my sister only said something about a little child that was born there, and the teacher was said to be the godfather.

112   Note that in this story the indecent scene is inserted at the wedding festivities, where it is just as appropriate as at the end, for the attentive reader will long ago have observed that it could also have taken place in the bathing-cabin. Actually, things have happened as they usually do in dreams: the final thought in a long series of dream-images contains precisely what the first

image in the series was trying to represent. The censor pushes the complex away as long as possible by means of ever-renewed symbolical disguises, displacements, bowdlerizations, etc. Nothing happens in the bathing-cabin, there is no piggyback in the water, on landing it is not on the teacher's back that the girls sit, it is another pair who get married, another girl has a child in the barn, and the teacher is only—godfather. But all these situations and images lend themselves to representing the wish for coitus. Behind all these metamorphoses the action nevertheless takes place, and the result is the birth staged at the end.

113 (3) Marie said: the teacher had a wedding with his wife, and afterwards they went to the Crown and danced together. Marie said all sorts of other wild things which I must not tell or write about, it is too embarrassing.

114 Here pretty well everything is too improper to be told. Note that the wedding takes place with the "wife."

115 (4) The teacher and Marie went bathing, and he asked Marie if she wanted to come along too. She said yes. When they had gone out together they met Lina, and the teacher asked if she wanted to come with them. And they went further out. Then I heard that she said the teacher said that Lina and she were his favourite pupils. She also told us that the teacher was in his bathing-dress. Then they went to a wedding and the bride got a little child.

116 The personal relationship to the teacher is strongly emphasized ("favourite pupils"), likewise the inadequate clothing ("bathing-dress").

117 (5) Marie and Lina went bathing with the teacher. When Marie and Lina and the teacher had swum a little way, Marie said, "Teacher, I can't go any further, my foot hurts me." The teacher told her to sit on his back and Marie did so. Then a little steamer came along and the teacher got into the ship. The teacher had two ropes with him and tied the children to the ship. Then they all went to Z. and got out there. The teacher bought himself a night-shirt and put it on and the children put a towel over them. Teacher had a bride and they were in a barn. The two children were also with the teacher and his bride in the barn and they danced. I must not write the other thing for it is too awful.

118 Here Marie sits on the teacher's back. The teacher fastens the two children to the ship with ropes, from which it can be

seen how easily "ship" is substituted for "teacher." The night-shirt again emerges as the article of clothing. It was the teacher's own wedding, and what is improper comes after the dance.

119   (6: Lina.) The teacher went bathing with the whole school. Marie could not find any room, and she cried. The teacher then told Marie she could come into his cabin.

"I must leave out something here and there," said my sister, "for it is a long story." But she told me something more which I must tell in order to speak the truth. When they were in the water the teacher asked Marie if she would like to swim across the lake with him. She answered that if I came she would come too. Then we swam about halfway. Marie got tired and the teacher pulled her by a cord. At K. they went on shore and from there to Z. All this time the teacher is supposed to have been dressed as for swimming. There we met a friend who was having a wedding. We were invited to it by this friend. After the feast there was a honeymoon trip, and we went to Milan. We had to sleep one night in a barn and there something happened which I must not tell. The teacher said we were his favourite pupils, and he also kissed Marie.

120   The excuse "I must leave out something here and there" re-places the undressing scene. Special emphasis is laid on the teacher's inadequate clothing. The journey to Milan is a typical honeymoon trip. This passage likewise seems to be an independent fantasy due to inner participation. Marie clearly figures as the loved one.

121   (7) The whole school and teacher went bathing. They all went into a room. Teacher also. Only Marie could find no room, so the teacher said to her, "I still have room." She went. Then the teacher said, "Lie on my back, I will swim out into the lake with you." I must not write any more, for it is so improper that I can hardly even say it. Except for the improper part which followed I know nothing more of the dream.

122   This narrator is getting down to the facts. Already at the bathing-place Marie was to lie on the teacher's back. Logically enough the narrator does not know anything of the rest of the dream except the improper part.

123   (8) The whole school went bathing. Marie had no room and was invited into his cabin by the teacher. The teacher swam out with her and told her, straight, she was his darling or something like

that. When they came ashore at Z. a friend had just had a wedding and this friend invited them both in their bathing-costume. The teacher had found an old night-shirt and put it on over his swimming-pants. He also kissed Marie a lot and said he would not go home to his wife any more. They were both invited on the honeymoon trip. The journey went through Andermatt, where they could not find any place to sleep, and so had to sleep in the hay. A woman was there too, now comes the dreadful part, and it is not at all right to laugh and joke about something so serious. This woman got a little child, but I will not say any more for it is too dreadful.

124   The narrator is very downright ("he told her, straight, she was his darling," "he kissed her a lot" etc.). Her obvious indignation over the silly tattling tells us something special about her character. Subsequent investigations showed that this girl was the only one of all the witnesses who had been sexually enlightened by her mother.

Summary

125   So far as the interpretation of the dream is concerned, there is nothing for me to add; the children themselves have done all that is necessary, leaving practically nothing over for psychoanalytic interpretation. *The rumour has analysed and interpreted the dream.* So far as I know, rumour has not been investigated in this capacity up to now. Our case certainly makes it appear worth while to fathom the psychology of rumour from the psychoanalytic side. In presenting the material I have purposely restricted myself to the psychoanalytic point of view, though I do not deny that my material offers numerous openings for the invaluable researches of the followers of Stern, Claparède, and others.

126   The material enables us to understand the structure of the rumour, but psychoanalysis cannot rest satisfied with that. We need to know more about the why and the wherefore of the whole phenomenon. As we have seen, the teacher was greatly affected by the rumour and was left puzzled by the problem of its cause and effect. How can a dream, which is notoriously harmless and never means anything (teachers, as we know, also have a training in psychology), produce such effects, such malicious gossip? Faced with this question, the teacher seems to me to have hit instinctively on the right answer. The effect of the

dream can only be explained by its being "le vrai mot de la situation"; that is to say, it gave suitable expression to something that was already in the air. It was the spark which fell into the powder-barrel. Our material affords all the necessary proofs of this view. Throughout, I have drawn attention to the inner participation of Marie's schoolmates in her dream, and to the points of special interest where some of them have added their own fantasies or day-dreams. The class consisted of girls between the ages of twelve and thirteen, who were therefore in the midst of the prodromata of puberty. The dreamer herself was almost fully developed sexually and in this respect ahead of her class; she was the leader who gave the watchword for the unconscious and so detonated the sexual complexes lying dormant in her companions.

127   As can easily be understood, the whole affair was most distressing for the teacher. The supposition that this, precisely, was what the girls secretly intended is justified by the psychoanalytic axiom that actions are to be judged more by their results than by their conscious motives.[5] Accordingly, we would conjecture that Marie had been especially troublesome to her teacher. At first she liked this teacher most of all. In the course of the last six months, however, her position had changed. She had become dreamy and inattentive, she was afraid to go into the streets after dark because of bad men. On several occasions she talked about sex to her companions in a rather obscene way; her mother asked me anxiously how she was to explain the approaching menstruation to her daughter. Because of her behaviour she had forfeited the good opinion of her teacher, as was clearly evidenced for the first time by a bad report which she and some of her friends received a few days before the outbreak of the rumour. Their disappointment was so great that the girls indulged in all sorts of vengeful fantasies about the teacher; for instance, they might push him on to the rails so that the train would run over him. Marie was especially to the fore in these murderous fantasies. On the night following this great outburst of anger, when her former love for her teacher seemed quite forgotten, that repressed part of herself rose up in the dream, and fulfilled its wish for sexual union with the

5 Cf. my "Psychic Conflicts in a Child."

teacher—as compensation for the hate which had filled the day.[6] On waking, the dream became a subtle instrument of her hatred, because its wishful thinking was also that of her companions, as it always is in rumours of this kind. Revenge certainly had its triumph, but the recoil upon Marie herself was even more severe. Such is the rule when our impulses are given over to the unconscious. Marie was expelled from school, but on my report was allowed to return.

128   I am well aware that this short report is inadequate and unsatisfactory from the point of view of exact science. Had the original story been accurately verified we could have demonstrated quite clearly what we have now only been able to suggest. This case, therefore, merely poses a question, and it remains for more fortunate observers to collect really convincing evidence in this field.

6 [It may be not without significance that, used transitively, the word *aufsitzen*—literally, 'sit a person up'—means 'to deceive,' 'to make a fool of,' someone, or, as we might say today in this context, 'to take him for a ride.'—TRANS.]

MORTON PRINCE, "THE MECHANISM AND
INTERPRETATION OF DREAMS":
A CRITICAL REVIEW [1]

154   I hope that all colleagues and fellow workers who, following in Freud's footsteps, have investigated the problem of dreams, and have been able to confirm the basic principles of dream-interpretation, will forgive me if I pass over their corroborative work and speak instead of another investigation which, though it has led to less positive results, is for that reason the more suited to public discussion. A fact especially worth noting is that Morton Prince, thanks to his previous work and his deep insight into psychopathological problems, is singularly well equipped to understand the psychology inaugurated by Freud. I do not know whether Morton Prince has sufficient command of German to read Freud in the original, though this is almost a *sine qua non* for understanding him. But if he must rely only on writings in English, the very clear presentation of dream-analysis by Ernest Jones, in "Freud's Theory of Dreams," [2] would have given him all the necessary knowledge. Apart from that, there are already a large number of articles and reports by Brill and Jones, and recently also by Putnam,[3] Meyer, Hoch, Scripture, and others, which shed light on the various aspects of psycho-

1 [Originally published in the *Jahrbuch für psychoanalytische und psychopathologische Forschungen*, III (1911), 309–28. The article by Prince (1854–1929) was published in the *Journal of Abnormal Psychology* (Boston), V (1910), 139–95. For Prince's relations with the early psychoanalytical movement, see Jones, *Life and Work*, II, passim.—EDITORS.]

2 *American Journal of Psychology*, XXI (1910), 283ff.

3 I should not omit to mention that James J. Putnam, professor of neurology in Harvard Medical School, has tested and made medical use of psychoanalysis. (See Putnam, "Persönliche Erfahrungen mit Freuds psychoanalytischer Methode," 1911.) [And Putnam's "Personal Impressions of Sigmund Freud and His Work" (1909–10). Adolf Meyer, August Hoch, and Edward Wheeler Scripture also practised in America.—EDITORS.]

analysis (or "depth psychology," as Bleuler calls it). And, for full measure, there have been available for some time not only Freud's and my lectures at Clark University,[4] but several translations of our works as well, so that even those who have no knowledge of German would have had ample opportunity to familiarize themselves with the subject.

155 It was not through personal contact, of whose suggestive influence Professor Hoche [5] has an almost superstitious fear very flattering to us, but presumably through reading that Morton Prince acquired the necessary knowledge of analysis. As the German-speaking reader may be aware, Morton Prince is the author of a valuable book, *The Dissociation of a Personality,* which takes a worthy place beside the similar studies of Binet, Janet, and Flournoy.[6] Prince is also, of course, the editor of the *Journal of Abnormal Psychology,* in almost every issue of which questions of psychoanalysis are discussed without bias.

156 From this introduction the reader will see that I am not saying too much when I represent Morton Prince as an unprejudiced investigator with a firmly established scientific reputation and undisputed competence in judging psychopathological problems. Whereas Putnam is chiefly concerned with the therapeutic aspect of psychoanalysis and has discussed it with admirable frankness, Morton Prince is interested in a particularly controversial subject, namely, dream-analysis. It is here that every follower of Freud has lost his honourable name as a man of science in the eyes of German scientists. Freud's fundamental

4 [The lectures were first published (in English translation) in the *American Journal of Psychology,* XXI (1910). For Freud's, see "Five Lectures on Psycho-Analysis," Standard Edn., XI. The three lectures by Jung, entitled "The Association Method," were republished in *Collected Papers on Analytical Psychology* (1916). For the first two, "The Association Method" and "The Familial Constellations," see Vol. 2 in the *Collected Works;* the third, "Psychic Conflicts in a Child," appears in Vol. 17 in its later, revised form of 1946.—EDITORS.]

5 As is well known, Professor Hoche, of Freiburg im Breisgau, described Freud and his school as afflicted with epidemic insanity. Participants in the congress accepted this diagnosis without rebuttal and with applause. [Alfred E. Hoche, "Eine psychische Epidemie unter Ärzten," Versammlung Süd-West Deutscher Irrenärzte, Baden-Baden, May 1910. See Jones, *Life and Work,* II, 131.—EDITORS.]

6 It is especially to be regretted that the learned men—or to be more accurate, the men who today go in for learning—all too often have an interest which is merely national and stops at the frontier. It would be a great relief to psychoanalysts if more Binet, Janet, and Flournoy were read in Germany.

contribution, *The Interpretation of Dreams,* has been treated with irresponsible levity by the German critics. As usual, they were ready to hand with glib phrases like "brilliant mistake," "ingenious aberration," etc. But that any of the psychologists, neurologists, and psychiatrists should really get down to it and try out his wit on Freud's dream-interpretation was too much to expect.[7] Perhaps they did not dare to. I almost believe they did not dare, because the subject is indeed very difficult—less, I think, for intellectual reasons than on account of personal, subjective resistances. For it is just here that psychoanalysis demands a sacrifice which no other science demands of its adherents: ruthless self-knowledge. It needs to be repeated again and again that *practical and theoretical understanding of psychoanalysis is a function of analytical self-knowledge.* Where self-knowledge fails, psychoanalysis cannot flourish. This is a paradox only so long as people think that they know themselves. And who does not think that? In ringing tones of deepest conviction everyone assures us that he does. And yet it is simply not true, a childish illusion which is indispensable to one's self-esteem. There can be no doubt whatever that a doctor who covers up his lack of knowledge and ability with increased self-confidence will never be able to analyse, for otherwise he would have to admit the truth to himself and would become impossible in his own eyes.

157 We must rate it all the higher, then, when a scientist of repute, like Morton Prince, courageously tackles the problem and seeks to master it in his own way. We are ready to meet at any time the objections that spring from honest work of this kind. We have no answer only for those who are afraid of real work and are satisfied with making cheap academic speeches. But before taking up Prince's objections, we shall have a look at his field of inquiry and at his—in our sense—positive results. Prince worked through six dreams of a woman patient who was capable of different states of consciousness and could be examined in several of these states. He used interrogation under hypnosis as well as "free association." We learn that he had already analysed

---

7 Those who did so were the ones who openly sided with Freud. Isserlin, on the other hand, contented himself with criticizing the method *a priori*, having no practical knowledge of the matter. Bleuler did what he could, under the circumstances, to answer him ("Die Psychoanalyse Freuds," 1910).

several dozen dreams.[8] Prince found that the method of free association "enables us by the examination of a large number of dreams in the same person to search the whole field of the unconscious, and by comparison of all the dreams to discover certain persistent, conserved ideas which run through and influence the psychical life of the individual." [9] Using the "insane" psychoanalytic method, therefore, the American investigator was able to discover, in the realm of the unconscious, something that perceptibly influences psychic life. For him the "method" is a method after all, he is convinced that there is an unconscious and all the rest of it, without being in any way hypnotized by Freud personally.

158   Prince admits, further, that we must consider as dream-material "certain subconscious ideas of which the subject had not been aware" (p. 150), thus recognizing that the sources of dreams can lie in the unconscious. The following passage brings important and emphatic confirmation of this:

It was a brilliant stroke of genius that led Freud to the discovery that dreams are not the meaningless vagaries that they were previously supposed to be, but when interpreted through the method of psychoanalysis may be found to have a logical and intelligible meaning. This meaning, however, is generally hidden in a mass of symbolism which can only be unraveled by a searching investigation into the previous mental experiences of the dreamer. Such an investigation requires, as I have already pointed out, the resurrection of all the associated memories pertaining to the elements of the dream. When this is done the conclusion is forced upon us, I believe, that even the most fantastic dream may express some intelligent idea, though that idea may be hidden in symbolism. My own observations confirm those of Freud, so far as to show that running through each dream there is an intelligent *motive;* so that the dream can be interpreted as expressing some idea or ideas which the dreamer previously has entertained. At least all the dreams I have subjected to analysis justify this interpretation.

8 In order to give the reader some idea of the experience the psychoanalyst possesses of dream analysis I would mention that, on average, I analyse eight dreams per working day. That makes about two thousand a year. Similar figures probably hold good for most psychoanalysts. Freud himself has immense experience in analysing dreams.
9 "The Mechanism and Interpretation of Dreams," p. 145.

159   Prince is thus in a position to admit that dreams have a meaning, that the meaning is hidden in symbols, and that in order to find the meaning one needs the memory-material. All this confirms essential portions of Freud's dream interpretation, far more than the *a priori* critics have ever admitted. As a result of certain experiences Prince has also come to conceive hysterical symptoms "as possible symbolisms of hidden processes of thought." In spite of the views expressed in Binswanger's *Die Hysterie,* which might have prepared the ground, this has still not penetrated the heads of German psychiatrists.

160   I have, as I said, begun with Prince's affirmative statements. We now come to the deviations and objections (p. 151):

> I am unable to confirm [Freud's view] that every dream can be interpreted as "the imaginary fulfillment of a wish," which is the motive of the dream. That sometimes a dream can be recognized as the fulfillment of a wish there can be no question, but that every dream, or that the majority of dreams are such, I have been unable to verify, even after subjecting the individual to the most exhaustive analysis. On the contrary I find, if my interpretations are correct, that some dreams are rather the expression of the non-fulfillment of a wish; some seem to be that of the fulfillment of a fear or anxiety.

161   In this passage we have everything that Prince cannot accept. It should be added that the wish itself often seems to him not to be "repressed" and not to be so unconscious or important as Freud would lead us to expect. Hence Freud's theory that a repressed wish is the real source of the dream, and that it fulfils itself in the dream, is not accepted by Prince, because he was unable to see these things in his material. But at least he tried to see them, and the theory seemed to him worth a careful check, which is definitely not the case with many of our critics. (I should have thought that this procedure would be an unwritten law of academic decency.) Fortunately, Prince has also presented us with the material from which he drew his conclusions. We are thus in a position to measure our experience against his and at the same time to find the reasons for any misunderstanding. He has had great courage in exposing himself in this commendable way, for we now have an opportunity to compare our divergencies openly with his material, a procedure which will be instructive in every respect.

162   In order to show how it is that Prince was able to see only the formal and not the dynamic element of the dreams, we must examine his material in more detail. One gathers, from various indications in the material, that the dreamer was a lady in late middle age, with a grown-up son who was studying, and apparently that she was unhappily married (or perhaps divorced or separated). For some years she had suffered from an hysterical dissociation of personality, and, we infer, had regressive fantasies about two earlier love-affairs, which the author, perhaps owing to the prudery of the public, is obliged to hint at rather too delicately. He succeeded in curing the patient of her dissociation for eighteen months, but now things seem to be going badly again, for she remained anxiously dependent on the analyst, and he found this so tiresome that he twice wanted to send her to a colleague.

163   Here we have the well-known picture of an unanalysed and unadmitted transference, which, as we know, consists in the anchoring of the patient's erotic fantasies to the analyst. The six dreams are an illustrative excerpt from the analyst's struggle against the clinging transference of the patient.

164   *Dream 1:* C [the patient's dream-ego] was somewhere and saw an old woman who appeared to be a *Jewess.* She was holding a *bottle* and a *glass* and seemed to be drinking *whiskey;* then this woman changed into her own *mother,* who had the bottle and glass, and appeared likewise to be drinking whiskey; then the door opened and her *father* appeared. He had on her *husband's dressing-gown,* and he was holding two *sticks of wood* in his hand. [Pp. 147ff.]

165   Prince found, on the basis of copious and altogether convincing material,[10] that the patient regarded the temptation to drink, and also the temptations of "poor people" in general, as something very understandable. She herself sometimes took a little whiskey in the evening, and so did her mother. But there might be something wrong in it. "The dream scene is therefore the symbolical representation and justification of her own belief and answers the doubts and scruples that beset her mind" (p. 154). The second part of the dream, about the sticks, is certainly, according to Prince, a kind of wish-fulfilment, but he says it tells us nothing, since the patient had ordered fire-

10 For the practised analyst the dream itself is so clear that it can be read directly.

wood the evening before. Despite the trouble expended on it (eight pages of print) the dream has not been analysed thoroughly enough, for the two most important items—the whiskey-drinking and the sticks—remain unanalysed. If the author would follow up those "temptations," he would soon discover that the patient's scruples are at bottom of a far more serious nature than a spoonful of whiskey and two bundles of wood. Why is the father who comes in, condensed with the husband? How is the Jewess determined other than by a memory of the previous day? Why are the two sticks significant and why are they in the hand of the father? And so on. The dream has not been analysed. Unfortunately its meaning is only too clear to the psychoanalyst. It says very plainly: "If I were this poor Jewess, whom I saw on the previous day, I would not resist temptation (just as mother and father don't—a typical infantile comparison!), and then a man would come into my room with firewood—naturally to warm me up." This, briefly, would be the meaning. The dream contains all that, only the author's analysis has discreetly stopped too soon. I trust he will forgive me for indiscreetly breaking open the tactfully closed door, so that it may clearly be seen what kind of wish-fulfilments, which "one cannot see," hide behind conventional discretion and medical blindness to sex.

166   *Dream 2:* A hill—she was toiling up the hill; one could hardly get up; had the sensation of some one, or thing, following her. She said, *"I must not show that I am frightened, or this thing will catch me."* Then she came where it was lighter, and she could see two clouds or *shadows,* one black and one red, and she said, "My God, it is *A and B!* If I don't have help I am lost." (She meant that she would change again—i.e., relapse into dissociated personalities.) She began to call "Dr. Prince! Dr. Prince!" and you were there and laughed, and said, "Well, you will have to fight the damned thing yourself." Then she woke up *paralysed* with fright. [P. 156.]

167   As the dream is very simple, we can dispense with any further knowledge of the analytical material. But Prince cannot see the wish-fulfilment in this dream, on the contrary he sees in it the "fulfilment of a fear." He commits the fundamental mistake of once again confusing the manifest dream-content with the unconscious dream-thought. In fairness to the author it should be remarked that in this case the repetition of the mistake was the

more excusable since the crucial sentence ("Well, you will have to fight the damned thing yourself") is really very ambiguous and misleading. Equally ambiguous is the sentence "I must not show that I am frightened," etc., which, as Prince shows from the material, refers to the thought of a relapse into the illness, since the patient was *frightened* of a relapse.

168   But what does "frightened" mean? We know that it is far more convenient for the patient to be ill, because recovery brings with it a great disadvantage: she would lose her analyst. The illness reserves him, as it were, for her needs. With her interesting illness, she has obviously offered the analyst a great deal, and has received from him a good deal of interest and patience in return. She certainly does not want to give up this stimulating relationship, and for this reason she is afraid of remaining well and secretly hopes that something weird and wonderful will befall her so as to rekindle the analyst's interest. Naturally she would do anything rather than admit that she really had such wishes. But we must accustom ourselves to the thought that in psychology there are things which the patient simultaneously knows and does not know. Things which are apparently quite unconscious can often be shown to be conscious in another connection, and actually to have been known. Only, they were not known in their true meaning. Thus, the true meaning of the wish which the patient could not admit was not directly accessible to her consciousness, which is why we call this true meaning not conscious, or "repressed." Put in the brutal form "I will have symptoms in order to re-arouse the interest of the analyst," it cannot be accepted, true though it is, for it is too hurtful; but she could well allow a few little associations and half-smothered wishes to be discerned in the background, such as reminiscences of the time when the analysis was so interesting, etc.

169   The sentence "I must not show that I am frightened" therefore means in reality "I must not show that I would really like a relapse because keeping well is too much trouble." "If I don't have help, I am lost" means "I hope I won't be cured too quickly or I cannot have a relapse." Then, at the end, comes the wish-fulfilment: "Well, you will have to fight the damned thing yourself." The patient keeps well only out of love for the analyst. If he leaves her in the lurch she will have a relapse, and it will

75

be his fault for not helping her. But if she has a relapse she will have a renewed and more intense claim on his attention, and this is the point of the whole manœuvre. It is altogether typical of dreams that the wish-fulfilment is always found where it seems most impossible to the conscious mind. The fear of a relapse is a symbol that needs analysing, and this the author has forgotten, because he took the fear, like the whiskey-drinking and the sticks, at its face value, instead of examining it sceptically for its genuineness. His colleague Ernest Jones's excellent work *On the Nightmare* [11] would have informed him of the wishful character of these fears. But, as I know from my own experience, it is difficult for a beginner to remain conscious of all the psychoanalytic rules all the time.

170   *Dream 3:* She was in the rocky path of Watts's,[12] barefooted, stones hurt her feet, few clothes, cold, could hardly climb that path; she saw you there, and she called on you to help her, and you said, "I cannot help you, you must help yourself." She said, "I can't, I can't." "Well, you have got to. Let me see if I cannot hammer it into your head." You picked up a stone and hammered her head, and with every blow you said, "I can't be bothered, I can't be bothered." And every blow sent a weight down into her heart so she felt heavy-hearted. She woke and I saw you pounding with a stone; you looked cross. [Pp. 159f.]

171   As Prince again takes the dream literally, he can see in it merely the "non-fulfillment of a wish." Once again it must be emphasized that Freud has expressly stated that the true *dream-thoughts are not identical with the manifest dream-contents.* Prince has not discovered the true dream-thought simply because he stuck to the wording of the dream. Now, it is always risky to intervene without knowing the material oneself; one can make enormous blunders. But it may be that the material brought out by the author's analysis will be sufficient to give us a glimpse of the latent dream-thought. (Anyone who has experience will naturally have guessed the meaning of the dream long ago, for it is perfectly clear.)

172   The dream is built up on the following experience. On the previous morning the patient had begged the author for medical help and had received the answer by telephone: "I cannot

11 [Orig. 1910.—EDITORS.]   12 See Dream 5.

possibly come to see you today. I have engagements all the day
and into the evening. I will send Dr. W, you must not depend
on me" (p. 160). An unmistakable hint, therefore, that the analyst's time belonged also to others. The patient remarked: "I
didn't say anything about it, but it played ducks and drakes with
me the other night." She therefore had a bitter morsel to swallow. The analyst had done something really painful, which she,
as a reasonable woman, understood well enough—but not with
her heart. Before going to sleep she had thought: "I must not
bother him; I should think I would get that *into my head* after
a while" (p. 161). (In the dream it is actually hammered into
her head.) "If my heart was not like a *stone,* I should weep."
(She was hammered with a stone.)

173   As in the previous dream, it is stated that the analyst will not
help her any more, and he hammers this decision of his into her
head so that at every blow her heart became heavier. The situation that evening, therefore, is taken up too clearly in the manifest dream-content. In such cases we must always try to find
where a new element has been added to the situation of the
previous day; at this point we may penetrate into the real meaning of the dream. The painful thing is that the analyst will not
treat the patient any more, but in the dream she *is* treated,
though in a new and remarkable way. When the analyst hammers it into her head that he cannot let himself be tormented
by her chatter, he does it so emphatically that his psychotherapy
turns into an extremely intense form of physical treatment or
torture. This fulfils a wish which is far too shocking to be recognized in the decent light of day, although it is a very natural
and simple thought. Popular humour and all the evil tongues
that have dissected the secrets of the confessional and the con-
sulting-room know it.[13] Mephistopheles, in his famous speech
about Medicine,[14] guessed it too. It is one of those imperishable
thoughts which nobody knows and everybody has.

13 Analysis by rumour. Cf. supra, "A Contribution to the Psychology of Rumour."
14 ["Learn how to handle women, that make sure,
   Since all the aches and sighs that come to vex
   The tender sex
   The doctor knows one little place to cure.
   A bedside manner sets their hearts at ease,
   And then they're yours for treatment as you please."
                    —*Faust,* Part One, trans. by Wayne, p. 98.]

174   When the patient awoke she saw the analyst still carrying
out that movement: pounding [15] with a stone. To name an
action for a second time is to give it special prominence.[16] As in
the previous dream, the wish-fulfilment lies in the greatest disappointment.

175   It will no doubt be objected that I am reading my own corrupt fantasies into the dream, as is customary with the Freudian
school. Perhaps my esteemed colleague, the author, will be indig-
nant at my attributing such impure thoughts to his patient, or
at least will find it quite unjustified of me to draw such a far-
reaching conclusion from these scanty hints. I am well aware
that this conclusion, seen from the standpoint of yesterday's
science, looks almost frivolous. But hundreds of parallel experiences have shown me that the above data are really quite sufficient to warrant my conclusion, and with a certainty that meets
the most rigorous requirements. Those who have no experience
of psychoanalysis can have no idea how very probable is the
presence of an erotic wish and how extremely improbable is its
absence. The latter illusion is naturally due to moral sex-blind-
ness on the one hand, but on the other to the disastrous mistake
of thinking that consciousness is the whole of the psyche. This
does not, of course, apply to our esteemed author. I therefore
beg the reader: no moral indignation, please, but calm verification. This is what science is made with, and not with howls of
indignation, mockery, abuse, and threats, the weapons which
the spokesmen of German science use in arguing with us.

176   It would really be incumbent on the author to present all
the interim material which would finally establish the erotic
meaning of the dream. Though he has not done it for this
dream, everything necessary is said indirectly in the following
dreams, so that my above-mentioned conclusion emerges from
its isolation and will prove to be a link in a consistent chain.

177   *Dream 4:* [Shortly before the last dream the subject] dreamt that
she was in a great *ballroom,* where everything was very *beautiful.*
She was walking about, and a man came up to her and asked,
"Where is your escort?" She replied, "I am *alone.*" He then said,
"You cannot stay here, we do not want any *lone women.*" In the

---

15 A pounder is a pestle or club.
16 Cf. "A Contribution to the Psychology of Rumour," par. 106.

next scene she was in a *theater* and was going to sit down, when someone came and said the same thing to her: "You can't stay here, we do not want any *lone women* here." Then she was in ever so many different places, but wherever she went she had to leave because she was *alone; they* would not let her stay. Then she was in the street; there was a great crowd, and she saw her husband a little way ahead, and struggled to get to him through the crowd. When she got quite near she saw . . . [what we may interpret as a symbolical representation of happiness, says Prince.] Then sickness and nausea came over her and she thought there was no place for her there either. [P. 162.]

178   The gap in the dream is a praiseworthy piece of discretion and will certainly please the prudish reader, but it is not science. Science admits no such considerations of decency. Here it is simply a question of whether Freud's maligned theory of dreams is right or not, and not whether dream-texts sound nice to immature ears. Would a gynaecologist suppress the illustration of the female genitalia in a textbook of midwifery on grounds of decency? On p. 164 of this analysis we read: "The analysis of this scene would carry us too far into the intimacy of her life to justify our entering upon it." Does the author really believe that in these circumstances he has any scientific right to speak about the psychoanalytic dream-theory, when he withholds essential material from the reader for reasons of discretion? By the very fact of reporting his patient's dream to the world he has violated discretion as thoroughly as possible, for every analyst will see its meaning at once: what the dreamer instinctively hides most deeply cries out loudest from the unconscious. For anyone who knows how to read dream-symbols all precautions are in vain, the truth will out. We would therefore request the author, if he doesn't want to strip his patient bare the next time, to choose a case about which he can say everything.

179   Despite his medical discretion this dream too, which Prince denies is a wish-fulfilment, is accessible to understanding. The end of the dream betrays, despite the disguise, the patient's violent resistance to sexual relations with her husband. The rest is all wish-fulfilment: she becomes a "lone woman" who is socially somewhat beyond the pale. The feeling of loneliness ("she feels that she cannot be alone any more, that she must have company") is fittingly resolved by this ambiguous situation: there

are "lone women" who are not so alone as all that, though certainly they are not tolerated everywhere. This wish-fulfilment naturally meets with the utmost resistance, until it is made clear that in case of necessity the devil, as the proverb says, eats even flies—and this is in the highest degree true of the libido. This solution, so objectionable to the conscious mind, seems thoroughly acceptable to the unconscious. One has to know what the psychology of a neurosis is in a patient of this age; psychoanalysis requires us to take people as they really are and not as they pretend to be. Since the great majority of people want to be what they are not, and therefore believe themselves identical with the conscious or unconscious ideal that floats before them, the individual is blinded by mass suggestion from the start, quite apart from the fact that he himself feels different from what he really is. This rule has the peculiarity of being true of everybody else, but never of the person to whom it is being applied.

180   I have set forth the historical and general significance of this fact in a previous work,[17] so I can spare myself the trouble of discussing it here. I would only remark that, to practise psychoanalysis, one must subject one's ethical concepts to a total revision. It is a requirement which explains why psychoanalysis becomes intelligible to a really serious person only gradually and with great difficulty. It needs not only intellectual but, to an even greater extent, moral effort to understand the meaning of the method, for it is not just a medical method like vibromassage or hypnosis, but something of much wider scope, that modestly calls itself "psychoanalysis."

181   *Dream 5:* She dreamt that she was in a dark, gloomy, rocky place, and she was walking with difficulty, as she always does in her dreams, over this rocky path, and all at once the place was filled with cats. She turned in terror to go back, and there in her path was a frightful creature like a wild man of the woods. His hair was hanging down his face and neck; he had a sort of skin over him for covering; his legs and arms were bare and he had a club. A wild figure. Behind him were hundreds of men like him—the whole place was filled with them, so that in front were cats and behind were wild men. The man said to her that she would have to go forward

17 *Symbols of Transformation.* [The first part of the original, *Wandlungen und Symbole der Libido,* appeared in the same issue of the *Jahrbuch* as the present article.—Editors.]

through those cats, and that if she made a sound they would all
come down on her and smother her, but if she went through them
without making a sound she would never again feel any regret
about the past . . . [mentioning certain specific matters which included two particular systems of ideas known as the Z and Y complexes, all of which had troubled her, adds the author]. She realized
that she must choose between death from the wild men and the
journey over the cats, so she started forward. Now, in her dream of
course she had to step on the cats [the subject here shivers and shud-
ders], and the horror of knowing that they would come on her if
she screamed caused her to make such an effort to keep still that the
muscles of her throat contracted in her dream [they actually did
contract, I could feel them, says Prince]. She waded through the
cats without making a sound, and then she saw her mother and
tried to speak to her. She reached out her hands and tried to say
"O mamma!" but she could not speak, and then she woke up feeling nauseated, frightened, and fatigued, and wet with perspiration.
Later, after waking, when she tried to speak, she could only whisper.
[Pp. 164f. A footnote adds: "She awoke with complete aphonia,
which persisted until relieved by appropriate suggestion."]

182   Prince sees this dream partly as a wish-fulfilment, because
the dreamer did after all walk over the cats. But he thinks:
"The dream would rather seem to be principally a symbolical
representation of her idea of life in general, and of the moral
precepts with which she has endeavoured to inspire herself, and
which she has endeavoured to live up to in order to obtain happiness" (p. 168).

183   That is not the meaning of the dream, as anyone can see
who knows anything of dreams. The dream has not been analysed at all. We are merely told that the patient had a phobia
about cats. What that means is not analysed. The treading on
the cats is not analysed. The wild man wearing the skin is not
analysed, and there is no analysis of the skin and the club. The
erotic reminiscences Z and Y are not described. The significance
of the aphonia is not analysed. Only the rocky path at the beginning is analysed a little: It comes from a painting by Watts,
"Love and Life." A female figure (Life) drags herself wearily
along the rocky path, accompanied by the figure of Love. The
initial image in the dream corresponds exactly to this picture,
"minus the figure of Love," as Prince remarks. Instead there
are the cats, as the dream shows and as we remark. This means

that the cats symbolize love. Prince has not seen this; had he studied the literature he would have discovered from one of my earlier publications that I have dealt in detail with the question of cat phobia.[18] There he would have been informed of this conclusion and could have understood the dream and the cat phobia as well.

184   For the rest, the dream is a typical anxiety dream which, in consequence, *must* be regarded from the standpoint of the sexual theory, unless Prince succeeds in proving to us that the sexual theory of anxiety is wrong. Owing to the complete lack of any analysis I refrain from further discussion of the dream, which is indeed very clear and pretty. I would only point out that the patient has succeeded in collecting a symptom (aphonia) which captured the interest of the analyst, as she reckoned it would. It is evident that one cannot criticize the dream-theory on the basis of analyses which are not made; this is merely the method of our German critics.

185   *Dream 6:* This dream occurred twice on succeeding nights. She dreamed she was in the same rocky, dark path she is always in—Watts's path—but with trees besides (there are always trees, or a hillside, or a canyon). The *wind* was blowing very hard, and she could hardly walk on account of something, as is always the case. Someone, a *figure,* came rushing past her with his hand over his (or her) eyes. This figure said, *"Don't look, you will be blinded."* She was at the entrance of a great *cave;* suddenly it *flashed light* in the cave like a flashlight picture, and there, down on the ground *you* were lying, and you were *bound round and round* with bonds of some kind, and your clothes were torn and dirty, and your face was covered with blood, and you looked terribly anguished; and all over you there were just hundreds of little gnomes or pigmies or brownies, and they were *torturing you.* Some of them had axes, and were chopping on your legs and arms, and some were sawing you. Hundreds of them had little things like joss-sticks, but shorter, which were red hot at the ends, and they were jabbing them into you. It was something like Gulliver and the little creatures running over him. You saw C, and you said, "O Mrs. C, for heaven's sake get me out of this damned hole." (You always swear in C's dreams.) She was horrified, and said, "O Dr. Prince, I am coming," but she *could not move,* she was rooted to the spot; and then it all went away,

[18] ["Association, Dream, and Hysterical Symptoms" (orig. 1906) in *Experimental Researches,* Coll. Works, Vol. 2.—Editors.]

everything became black, as if she were *blinded,* and then it would flash again and illuminate the cave, and she would see again. This happened three or four times in the dream. She kept saying, "I am coming," and *struggled to move,* and she woke up saying it. In the same way *she could not move when she woke up, and she could not see.* [Pp. 170f.]

186   The author does not report the details of the analysis of this dream, "in order not to weary the reader." He gives only the following résumé:

The dream proved to be a symbolic representation of the subject's conception of life (the rocky path), of her dread of the future, which for years she has said she dared not face; of her feeling that the future was "blind," in that she could not "see anything ahead"; of the thought that she would be overwhelmed, "lost," "swept away" if she looked into and realized this future, *and she must not look.* And yet there are moments in life when she realizes vividly the future; and so in the dream one of these moments is when she looks into the cave (the future), and in the flash of light the realization comes—she sees her son (metamorphosed through substitution of another person) tortured, as she has thought of him tortured, and handicapped (bound) by the moral "pin pricks" of life. Then follows the symbolic representation (paralysis) of her utter "helplessness" to aid either him or anyone else or alter the conditions of her own life. Finally follow the prophesied consequences of this realization. She is overcome by blindness and to this extent the dream is a fulfillment of a fear. [P. 171.]

187   The author says in conclusion: "In this dream, as in the others, we find no 'unacceptable' and 'repressed wish,' no 'conflict' with 'censoring thoughts,' no 'compromise,' no 'resistance' and no 'disguise' in the dream-content to deceive the dreamer —elements and processes fundamental in the Freud school of psychology" (p. 173).

188   From this devastating judgment we shall delete the words "as in the others," for the other dreams are analysed so inadequately that the author has no right to pronounce such a judgment on the basis of the preceding "analyses." Only the last dream remains to substantiate this judgment, and we shall therefore look at it rather more closely.

189   We shall not linger over the constantly recurring symbol of

the painting by Watts, in which the figure of Love is missing and was replaced by the cats in dream 5. Here it is replaced by a figure who warns the patient not to look or she will be "blinded." Now comes another very remarkable image: the analyst bound round and round with bonds, his clothes torn and dirty, his face covered with blood—the Gulliver situation. Prince remarks that it is the patient's son who is in this agonizing situation, but withholds further details. Where the bonds, the bloody face, the torn clothes come from, what the Gulliver situation means—of all this we learn nothing. Because the patient "must not look into the future," the cave signifies the future, remarks Prince. But why is the future symbolized by a cave? The author is silent. How comes it that the analyst is substituted for the son? Prince mentions the patient's helplessness with regard to the situation of the son, and observes that she is just as helpless with regard to the analyst, for she does not know how to show her gratitude. But these are, if I may say so, two quite different kinds of helplessness, which do not sufficiently explain the condensation of the two persons. An essential and unequivocal *tertium comparationis* is lacking. All the details of the Gulliver situation, especially the red-hot joss-sticks, are left unanalysed. The highly significant fact that the analyst himself suffers hellish tortures is passed over in complete silence.

¹⁹⁰ In Dream 3 the analyst pounded the patient on the head with a stone, and this torture seems to be answered here, but swelled out into a hellish fantasy of revenge. Without doubt these tortures were thought up by the patient and intended for her analyst (and perhaps also for her son); that is what the dream says. This fact needs analysing. If the son is really "tortured by the moral pin pricks of life," we definitely require to know why in the dream the patient multiplies this torture a hundred-fold, brings the son (or the analyst) into the Gulliver situation and then puts Gulliver in the "damned hole." Why must the analyst swear in the dreams? Why does the patient step into the analyst's shoes and say she is unable to bring help, when really the situation is the other way round?

¹⁹¹ Here the way leads down into the wish-fulfilling situation. But the author has not trodden this path; he has either omitted to ask himself any of these questions or answered them much too

superficially, so that this analysis too must be disqualified as "unsatisfactory." [19]

192   With this the last prop for a criticism of the dream-theory collapses. We must require of a critic that he carry out his investigations just as thoroughly as the founder of the theory, and that he should at least be able to explain the main points of the dream. But in the author's analyses, as we have seen, the most important items are brushed aside. You cannot produce psychoanalysis out of a hat, as everyone knows who has tried; *unumquemque movere lapidem* is nearer the truth.

*

193   Only after the conclusion of this review did I see the criticism which Ernest Jones [20] lavished on Morton Prince's article. We learn from Prince's reply that he *does not claim to have used the psychoanalytic method*. In that case he might fairly have refrained from criticizing the findings of psychoanalysis, it seems to me. His analytical methods, as the above examples show, are so lacking in scientific thoroughness that the conclusions he reaches offer no basis for a serious criticism of Freud's dream-theory. The rest of his remarks, culminating in the admission that he will never be able to see eye to eye with the psychoanalytic school, do not encourage me to make further efforts to explain the problems of dream-psychology to him or to discuss his reply. I confine myself to expressing my regret that he has even gone to the length of denying the scientific training and scientific thinking of his opponents.

19 The dream is a typical fantasy of revenge for scorned love and contains in the torture (as in the pounding) scene the boundless gratitude of the patient. Hence the mysterious scene in the cave, which is so scandalous that she will be struck blind at the sight of it. Proof of this can be found in the details of the cave scene.
20 "Remarks on Dr. Morton Prince's article, 'The Mechanism and Interpretation of Dreams' " (1910–11).

ON THE CRITICISM OF PSYCHOANALYSIS [1]

194   It is a well-known fact to the psychoanalyst that laymen, even those with relatively little education, are able to understand the nature and rationale of psychoanalysis without undue intellectual difficulty. It is the same with educated people, be they scholars, business-men, journalists, artists, or teachers. They can all understand the truths of psychoanalysis. They also understand very well why psychoanalysis cannot be expounded in the same convincing way as a mathematical proposition. Everyone of common sense knows that a psychological proof must necessarily be different from a physical one, and that each branch of science can only offer proofs that are suited to its material. It would be interesting to know just what kind of empirical proof our critics expect, if not proof on the evidence of the empirical facts. Do these facts exist? We point to our observations. Our critics, however, simply say No. What, then, are we to offer if our factual observations are flatly denied? Under these circumstances we would expect our critics to study the neuroses and psychoses as thoroughly as we have done (quite independently of the method of psychoanalysis), and to put forward facts of an essentially different kind concerning their psychological determination. We have waited for this for more than ten years. Fate has even decreed that all investigators in this field who have worked independently of the discoverer of the new theory, but as thoroughly, have arrived at the same results as Freud; and that those who have taken the time and trouble to acquire the necessary knowledge under a psychoanalyst have also gained an understanding of these results.

195   In general, we must expect the most violent resistance from medical men and psychologists, chiefly because of scientific

1 [Translated from "Zur Kritik über Psychoanalyse," *Jahrbuch für psychoanalytische und psychopathologische Forschungen* (Leipzig), II (1910), 743–46.—EDITORS.]

prejudices based on a different way of thinking to which they obstinately adhere. Our critics, unlike earlier ones, have progressed inasmuch as they try to be more serious and to strike a more moderate note. But they commit the mistake of criticizing the psychoanalytic method as though it rested on *a priori* principles, whereas in reality it is purely empirical and totally lacking in any final theoretical framework. All we know is that it is simply the quickest way to find facts which are of importance for our psychology, but which, as the history of psychoanalysis shows, can also be discovered in other more tedious and complicated ways. We would naturally be happy if we possessed an analytical technique which led us to the goal even more quickly and reliably than the present method. Our critics, however, will scarcely be able to help us towards a more suitable technique, and one that corresponds better to the assumptions of psychology up till now, merely by contesting our findings. So long as the question of the facts is not settled, all criticism of the method hangs in the air, for concerning the ultimate secrets of the association process our opponents know as little as we do. It should be obvious to every thinking person that what matters is simply and solely the empirical facts. If criticism confines itself to the method, it may easily come one day to deny the existence of facts merely because the method of finding them betrays certain theoretical defects—a standpoint that would carry us happily back to the depths of the Middle Ages. In this respect our critics commit grave mistakes. It is the duty of intelligent people to point them out, for to err is human.

196   Occasionally, however, the criticism assumes forms which arouse the interest of the psychological worker in the highest degree, since the scientific endeavour of the critic is thrust into the background in the most surprising way by symptoms of personal participation. Such critics make a valuable contribution to the knowledge of the personal undercurrents beneath so-called scientific criticism. We cannot deny ourselves the pleasure of making such a *document humain* accessible to a wider public.

*

Review by Kurt Mendel [2] of an Exposition of the Freudian Standpoint

The present reviewer, who has read many works of Freud and his followers, and has *himself had practical experience of psychoanalysis*,[3] must admit that he finds many things in this doctrine utterly repugnant, especially the latest additions concerning anal eroticism and the sexuality of children. After perusing the work under review,[4] he stepped up to his youngest child, lying there innocently in his cot, and spoke as follows: "Poor little boy! I fancied you were pure and chaste, but now I know that you are depraved and full of sin! 'From the first day of your existence you have led a sexual life' (p. 184); now you are an exhibitionist, a fetishist, a sadist, a masochist, an anal-erotic, an onanist—in short, you are 'polymorphous-perverse' (p. 185). 'There is scarcely a Don Juan among grown-ups whose erotic fantasies could be compared with the products of your infant brain' (p. 185). How, indeed, could it be otherwise? For you are corrupt from birth. Your father has the reputation of being unusually tidy and economical, and the Freudians say he is stubborn because he won't give full acceptance to their teachings. Unusually tidy, economical, and stubborn! A hopeless anal-erotic, therefore! (Cf. Freud, "Charakter und Analerotik," *Psych.-neur. Wochenschr.* IX: 51.) As for your mother, she cleans out the house every four weeks. 'Cleaning, and particularly spring-cleaning, is the specific female reaction to suppressed anal eroticism' (Sadger, "Analerotik und Analcharakter," *Die Heilkunde,* Feb. 1910). You are a congenital anal-erotic from your father's and your mother's side! And a little while ago, before going to bed, you would not 'empty the bowels when you were put on the pot, because you want to derive extra pleasure from defecation and therefore enjoy holding back your stool.' Previously your father simply told your mother on such occasions: 'The boy is constipated, give him a pill!' Pfui! How shamelessly perverse I was then, a regular pimp and corrupter of youth! You'll get no good-night kiss from me any more, for a caress like that would only 'arouse your sexuality' (p. 191). And don't say your evening prayer to me again: 'I am small, my heart is pure'; [5] that would be a lie; you are dissipated, an exhibitionist, fetishist, sadist, mas-

---

[2] In *Neurologisches Centralblatt* (Leipzig), XXIX : 6 (March 16, 1910).
[3] My italics.—C. G. J.
[4] J. A. Haslebacher, "Psychoneurosen und Psychoanalyse," *Correspondenzblatt für Schweizer Ärzte* (Basel), XL:7 (March 1, 1910), 184–96.
[5] "Ich bin klein, mein Herz ist rein."

ochist, anal-erotic, onanist, 'polymorphous-perverse'—through me, through your mother, and through yourself! Poor little boy!"

Freudians! I have repeatedly asserted that your teachings have opened up many new and valuable perspectives. But for heaven's sake make an end of your boundless exaggerations and nonsensical fantasies! Instead of puns, give us proofs! Instead of books that read like comics, give us serious works to be taken seriously! Prove to me the truth of your squalid and slanderous statement (p. 187): "There is but one form of love, and that is erotic love"! Do not plunge our most sacred feelings, our love and respect for our parents and our happy love for our children, into the mire of your fantasies by the continual imputation of sordid sexual motives! Your whole argument culminates in the axiom: "Freud has said it, therefore it is so!" But I say with Goethe, the son of an anal-erotic (Sadger, op. cit.):

> "A man who speculates
> Is like a beast upon a barren heath
> Led round in circles by an evil sprite,
> While all around lie pastures green and bright."

CONCERNING PSYCHOANALYSIS [1]

Küsnacht, 28 January 1912

To the Editor.

Sir,

197   Thank you for kindly inviting me to publish in your columns an epilogue to the series of articles in the *Neue Zürcher Zeitung*. Such an epilogue could only be a defence either of the scientific truth which we think we can discern in psychoanalysis, and which has been so heavily attacked, or of our own scientific qualities. The latter defence offends against good taste, and is unworthy of anyone dedicated to the service of science. But a defence of the first kind can be carried out only if the discussion takes an objective form, and if the arguments used arise from a careful study of the problem, practical as well as theoretical. I am ready to argue with opponents like this, though I prefer to do so in private; I have, however, also done it in public, in a scientific journal. [2]

198   I shall not reply, either, to scientific criticism the essence of which is: "The method is morally dangerous, therefore the theory is wrong," or: "The facts asserted by the Freudians do not exist but merely spring from the morbid fantasy of these so-called researchers, and the method used for discovering these facts is in itself logically at fault." No one can assert *a priori* that certain facts do not exist. This is a scholastic argument, and it is superfluous to discuss it.

---

1 [Translated from "Zur Psychoanalyse," *Wissen und Leben* (Zurich; former title of the *Neue Schweizer Rundschau*), V (1912), 711–14. An introductory editorial note stated: "A series of communications pro and con Freudian theories in the *Neue Zürcher Zeitung* seems to prove that remarkable misunderstanding and prejudice with respect to modern psychology are the rule with the general public. Since all this impassioned wrangling was more likely to confuse than to enlighten, we have asked Dr. Karl Jung (*sic*) for a few closing words, which should be the more welcome for calming ruffled tempers."—EDITORS.]

2 [See the preceding article.—EDITORS.]

199   It is repugnant to me to make propaganda for the truth and
to defend it with slogans. Except in the Psychoanalytical Society
and in the Swiss Psychiatric Society I have never yet given
a public lecture without first having been asked to do so; similarly, my article in Rascher's Yearbook [3] was written only at the
request of the editor, Konrad Falke. I do not thrust myself upon
the public. I shall therefore not enter the arena now in order to
engage in barbarous polemics on behalf of a scientific truth.
Prejudice and the almost boundless misunderstanding we are
faced with can certainly prevent progress and the spread of
scientific knowledge for a long time, and this is perhaps a necessity of mass psychology to which one has to submit. If this truth
does not speak for itself, it is a poor truth and it is better for it
to perish. But if it is an inner necessity, it will make its way,
even without battle-cries and the martial blast of trumpets, into
the hearts of all straight-thinking and realistic persons and so
become an essential ingredient of our civilization.

200   The sexual indelicacies which unfortunately occupy a necessarily large place in many psychoanalytic writings are not to be
blamed on psychoanalysis itself. Our very exacting and responsible medical work merely brings these unlovely fantasies to
light, but the blame for the existence of these sometimes repulsive and evil things must surely lie with the mendaciousness
of our sexual morality. No intelligent person needs to be told
yet again that the psychoanalytic method of education does not
consist merely in psychological discussions of sex, but covers
every department of life. The goal of this education, as I have
expressly emphasized in Rascher's Yearbook, is not that a man
should be delivered over helplessly to his passions but that he
should attain the necessary self-control. In spite of Freud's and
my assurances, our opponents want us to countenance "licentiousness" and then assert that we do so, regardless of what we
ourselves say. It is the same with the theory of neurosis—the
sexual or libido theory, as it is called. For years I have been
pointing out, both in my lectures and in my writings, that the
concept of libido is taken in a very general sense, rather like
the instinct of preservation of the species, and that in psycho-

[3] [*Neue Bahnen der Psychologie*, published in *Raschers Jahrbuch für Schweizer
Art und Kunst* (Zurich), 1912. Trans. as "New Paths in Psychology," *Two Essays
on Analytical Psychology*, pars. 407ff.—EDITORS.]

analytic parlance it definitely does not mean "localized sexual excitation" but all striving and willing that exceed the limits of self-preservation, and that this is the sense in which it is used. I have also recently expressed my views on these general ques tions in a voluminous work,[4] but our opponents wishfully decree that our views are as "grossly sexual" as their own. Our efforts to expound our psychological standpoint are quite use-less, as our opponents want this whole theory to resolve itself into unspeakable banality. I feel powerless in the face of this overwhelming demand. I can only express my sincere distress that, through a misunderstanding which confuses day with night, many people are preventing themselves from employing the extraordinary insights afforded by psychoanalysis for the benefit of their own ethical development. Equally I regret that, by thoughtlessly ignoring psychoanalysis, many people are blinding themselves to the profundity and beauty of the human soul.

201   No sensible person would lay it at the door of scientific re-search and its results that there are clumsy and irresponsible people who use it for purposes of hocus-pocus. Would anybody of intelligence lay the blame for the faults and imperfections in the execution of a method designed for the good of mankind on the method itself? Where would surgery be if one blamed its methods for every lethal outcome? Surgery is very dangerous indeed, especially in the hands of a fool. No one would trust himself to an unskilled surgeon or let his appendix be removed by a barber. So it is with psychoanalysis. That there are not only unskilled psychiatrists but also laymen who play about in an irresponsible way with psychoanalysis cannot be denied, any more than that there are, today as always, unsuitable doctors and unscrupulous quacks. But this fact does not entitle anyone to lump together science, method, researcher, and doctor in a wholesale condemnation.

202   I regret, Sir, having to bore you and the readers of your paper with these self-evident truths, and I therefore hasten to a conclusion. You must forgive me if my manner of writing is

[4] [Presumably *Wandlungen und Symbole der Libido*, Part I of which appeared in the *Jahrbuch* in 1911. Part II, the second chapter of which is devoted to the con-cept and the genetic theory of the libido, appeared early in 1912.—EDITORS.]

at times a little heated; but no one, perhaps, is so far above public opinion as not to be painfully affected by the frivolous discrediting of his honest scientific endeavours.

Yours, etc.,

DR. JUNG

THE SIGNIFICANCE OF THE FATHER IN THE DESTINY OF THE INDIVIDUAL [1]

Foreword to the Second Edition

This little essay, written seventeen years ago, ended with the words: "It is to be hoped that experience in the years to come will sink deeper shafts into this obscure territory, on which I have been able to shed but a fleeting light, and will discover more about the secret workshop of the daemon who shapes our fate." Experience in later years has indeed altered and deepened many things; some of them have appeared in a different light, and I have seen how the roots of the psyche and of fate go deeper than the "family romance," and that not only the children but the parents, too, are merely branches of one great tree. While I was working on the mother-complex in my book *Wandlungen und Symbole der Libido*,[2] it became clear to me what the deeper causes of this complex are; why not only the father, but the mother as well, is such an important factor in the child's fate: not because they themselves have this or that human failing or merit, but because they happen to be—by accident, so to speak—the human beings who first impress on the childish mind those mysterious and mighty laws which govern not only families but entire nations, indeed the whole of humanity. Not laws devised by the wit of man, but the laws and forces of nature, amongst which man walks as on the edge of a razor.

I am letting this essay appear in unaltered form. There is nothing in it that is actually wrong—merely too simple, too naïve. The

1 [First published as "Die Bedeutung des Vaters für das Schicksal des Einzelnen," *Jahrbuch für psychoanalytische und psychopathologische Forschungen* (Leipzig), I (1909), 155–73. This was translated by M. D. Eder under the present title and published in *Collected Papers on Analytical Psychology* (London and New York, 1916; 2nd edn., 1917). The German original of the article was reprinted (1909) as a pamphlet, and a second edition in this form appeared (Vienna, 1927) with a brief foreword. A third edition, much revised and expanded, with a new foreword, was published in 1949 (Zurich). The present version is a translation of the third edition. Passages which the author added to that version are given in pointed brackets ⟨ ⟩ in the text, while any of significance which they replaced, or which were omitted, are given in square brackets [ ] in the footnotes (as translated from the 1909 version).—EDITORS.]

2 [Revised (1952) and translated as *Symbols of Transformation*.—EDITORS.]

Horatian verse, which I then placed at the end, points to that deeper, darker background:

> "Scit Genius natale comes qui temperat astrum,
> Naturae deus humanae, mortalis in unum,
> Quodque caput, vultu mutabilis, albus et ater." [3]

C. G. J.

Küsnacht, December 1926

Foreword to the Third Edition

This essay was written nearly forty years ago, but this time I did not want to publish it in its original form. Since that time so many things have changed and taken on a new face that I felt obliged to make a number of corrections and additions to the original text. It was chiefly the discovery of the collective unconscious that raised new problems for the theory of complexes. Previously the personality appeared to be unique and as if rooted in nothing; but now, associated with the individually acquired causes of the complex, there was found to be a general human precondition, the inherited and inborn biological structure which is the instinctual basis of every human being. From it proceed, as throughout the whole animal kingdom, determining forces which inhibit or strengthen the more or less fortuitous constellations of individual life. Every normal human situation is provided for and, as it were, imprinted on this inherited structure, since it has happened innumerable times before in our long ancestry. At the same time the structure brings with it an inborn tendency to seek out, or to produce, such situations instinctively. A repressed content would indeed vanish into the void were it not caught and held fast in this pre-established instinctual substrate. Here are to be found those forces which offer the most obstinate resistance to reason and will, thus accounting for the conflicting nature of the complex.

I have tried to modify the old text in accordance with these discoveries and to bring it, in some degree, up to the level of our present knowledge.

C. G. J.

October 1948

3 "[(Why this should be so) only the Genius knows—that companion who rules the star of our birth, the god of human nature, mortal though he be in each single life, and changeful of countenance, white and black."—Horace, *Epistles*, II, ii, 187–89.—TRANS.]

The Fates lead the willing,
but drag the unwilling.

CLEANTHES

693   Freud has pointed out that the emotional relationship of the
child to the parents, and particularly to the father, is of a decisive
significance in regard to the content of any later neurosis. This
relationship is indeed the infantile channel along which the
libido [4] flows back when it encounters any obstacles in later
years, thus reactivating the long-forgotten psychic contents of
childhood. It is ever so in life when we draw back before too
great an obstacle, say the threat of some severe disappointment
or the risk of some too far-reaching decision. The energy stored
up for the solution of the task flows back and the old river-beds,
the obsolete systems of the past, are filled up again. A man dis-
illusioned in love falls back, as a substitute, upon some senti-
mental friendship [5] or false religiosity; if he is a neurotic he
regresses still further back to the childhood relationships he has
never quite forsaken, and to which even the normal person is
fettered by more than one chain—the relationship to father and
mother.

694   Every analysis carried out at all thoroughly shows this regression more or less plainly. One peculiarity which stands out in
the works of Freud is that the relationship to the father seems
to possess a special significance. ⟨This is not to say that the father
always has a greater influence on the moulding of the child's
fate than the mother. His influence is of a specific nature and
differs typically from hers.[6]⟩

695   The significance of the father in moulding the child's psyche
may be discovered in quite another field—the study of the family.[7] The latest investigations show the predominating influence
of the father's character in a family, often lasting for centuries.

[4] [Orig. footnote: Libido is what earlier psychologists called "will" or "tendency."
The Freudian expression is a denominatio a potiori. Jahrbuch, I (1909), 155.]
[5] [In orig., also: masturbation.]
[6] ⟨I have discussed this question on two occasions: Symbols of Transformation
(in regard to the son), and "Psychological Aspects of the Mother Archetype" (in
regard to the daughter).⟩
[7] Sommer, Familienforschung und Vererbungslehre (1907); Joerger, "Die Familie
Zero" (1905); Ziermer, "Genealogische Studien über die Vererbung geistiger
Eigenschaften" (1908).

The mother seems to play a less important role. If this is true of heredity, we may expect it to be true also of the psychological influences emanating from the father.[8] The scope of the problem has been widened by the researches of my pupil, Dr. Emma Fürst, on the similarity of reaction-type within families.[9] She conducted association tests on 100 persons coming from 24 families. From this extensive material, so far only the results for nine families and 37 persons (all uneducated) have been worked out and published. But the calculations already permit some valuable conclusions. The associations were classified on the Kraepelin-Aschaffenburg scheme as simplified and modified by me, and the difference was then calculated between each group of qualities in a given subject and the corresponding group in every other subject. We thus get mean figures of the differences in reaction-type.

Non-related men	5.9
Non-related women	6.0
Related men	4.1
Related women	3.8

696   Relatives, especially if they are women, therefore have on average a similar reaction-type. This means that the psychological attitude of relatives differs but slightly. Examination of the various relationships yielded the following results:

697   The mean difference for husband and wife amounts to 4.7%. But the dispersion value for this mean figure is 3.7, which is high, indicating that the mean of 4.7 is composed of a very wide range of figures: there are married couples with great similarity in reaction-type and others with less.

698   On the whole, fathers and sons, mothers and daughters, stand closer together:

Difference for fathers and sons:	3.1
Difference for mothers and daughters:	3.0

8 [*Orig.:* These experiences, and those gained more particularly in an analysis carried out conjointly with Dr. Otto Gross, have impressed upon me the soundness of this view.] [For Gross, cf. Jones, *Freud: Life and Work,* II, p. 33.—Editors.]
9 "Statistical Investigations on Word-Associations and on Familial Agreement in Reaction Type among Uneducated Persons" (orig. 1907).

699   Except for a few cases of married couples (where the difference dropped to 1.4), these are among the lowest figures. Fürst even had one case where a 45-year-old mother and her 16-year-old daughter differed by only 0.5. But it was just in this case that the mother and daughter differed from the father's reaction-type by 11.8. The father was a coarse, stupid man and a drinker; the mother went in for Christian Science. In accordance with this, mother and daughter exhibited an extreme value-predicate type of reaction,[10] which in my experience is an important sign of a conflicting relationship to the object. Value-predicate types show excessive intensity of feeling and thus betray an unadmitted but nonetheless transparent desire to evoke answering feelings in the experimenter. This view agrees with the fact that in Fürst's material the number of value-predicates increases with the age of the subject.

700   The similarity of reaction-type in children and parents provides matter for thought. For the association experiment is nothing other than a small segment of the psychological life of a man, and everyday life is at bottom an extensive and greatly varied association experiment; in principle we react in one as we do in the other. Obvious as this truth is, it still requires some reflection—and limitation. Take the case of the 45-year-old mother and her 16-year-old daughter: the extreme value-predicate type of the mother is without doubt the precipitate of a whole life of disappointed hopes and wishes. One is not in the least surprised at a value-predicate type here. But the 16-year-old daughter had not really lived at all; she was not yet married, and yet she reacted as if she were her mother and had endless disillusions behind her. She had her mother's attitude, and to that extent was identified with her mother. The mother's attitude was explained by her relationship to the father. But the daughter was not married to the father and therefore did not need this attitude. She simply took it over from the environmental influences and later on will try to adapt herself to the world under the influence of this family problem. To the extent that an ill-assorted marriage is unsuitable, the attitude resulting from it will be unsuitable too. In order to adapt, the girl in later

10 By this I mean reactions where the response to the stimulus-word is always a subjectively toned predicate instead of an objective relationship, e.g., *flower / nice, frog / horrible, piano / frightful, salt / bad, singing / sweet, cooking / useful.*

life will have to overcome the obstacles of her family milieu; if she does not, she will succumb to the fate to which her attitude predisposes her.

701   Clearly such a fate has many possibilities. The glossing over of the family problem and the development of the negative of the parental character may take place deep within, unnoticed by anyone, in the form of inhibitions and conflicts which she herself does not understand. Or, as she grows up, she will come into conflict with the world of actualities, fitting in nowhere, until one stroke of fate after another gradually opens her eyes to her own infantile, unadapted qualities. The source of the infantile disturbance of adaptation is naturally the emotional relation to the parents. It is a kind of psychic contagion, caused, as we know, not by logical truths but by affects and their physical manifestations.[11] In the most formative period between the first and fifth year all the essential characteristics, which fit exactly into the parental mould, are already developed, for experience teaches us that the first signs [12] of the later conflict between the parental constellation and the individual's longing for independence occur as a rule before the fifth year.

702   I would like to show, with the help of a few case-histories, how the parental constellation hinders the child's adaptation.[13]

Case 1

703   A well-preserved woman of 55, dressed poorly but carefully, with a certain elegance, in black; hair carefully arranged; a polite, rather affected manner, fastidious in speech, devout. The patient might be the wife of a minor official or shopkeeper. She informed me, blushing and dropping her eyes, that she was the divorced wife of a common peasant. She had come to the clinic on account of depression, night terrors, palpitations, and nervous twitches in the arms—typical features of a mild climacteric neurosis. To complete the picture, the patient added that she suffered from severe anxiety-dreams; some man was pursuing her, wild animals attacked her, and so on.

11 Vigouroux and Juquelier, *La Contagion mentale* (1904), ch. 6.
12 [*Orig.:* . . . of the struggle between repression and libido (Freud) . . .]
13 [*Orig.:* It must suffice to present only the chief events, i.e., those of sexuality.]

704   Her anamnesis began with the family history. (So far as possible I give her own words.) Her father was a fine, stately, rather corpulent man of imposing appearance. He was very happily married, for her mother worshipped him. He was a clever man, a master craftsman, and held a dignified position. There were only two children, the patient and an elder sister. The sister was the mother's and the patient the father's favourite. When she was five years old her father suddenly died of a stroke at the age of forty-two. She felt very lonely, and also that from then on she was treated by her mother and sister as the Cinderella. She noticed clearly enough that her mother preferred her sister to herself. The mother remained a widow, her respect for her husband being too great to allow her to marry a second time. She preserved his memory "like a religious cult" and taught her children to do likewise.

705   The sister married relatively young; the patient did not marry till she was twenty-four. She had never cared for young men, they all seemed insipid; her mind turned always to more mature men. When about twenty she became acquainted with a "stately" gentleman of over forty, to whom she was much drawn, but for various reasons the relationship was broken off. At twenty-four she got to know a widower who had two children. He was a fine, stately, rather corpulent man, with an imposing presence, like her father; he was forty-four. She married him and respected him enormously. The marriage was childless; his children by the first marriage died of an infectious disease. After four years of married life her husband died of a stroke. For eighteen years she remained his faithful widow. But at forty-six (just before the menopause) she felt a great need of love. As she had no acquaintances she went to a matrimonial agency and married the first comer, a peasant of about sixty who had already been twice divorced on account of brutality and perverseness; the patient knew this before marriage. She remained five unbearable years with him, then she also obtained a divorce. The neurosis set in a little later.

706   For the reader with psychological [14] experience no further elucidation is needed; the case is too obvious. I would only emphasize that up to her forty-sixth year the patient did nothing

---

14 [*Orig.*: psychanalytical.]

but live out a faithful copy of the milieu of her early youth.
The exacerbation of sexuality at the climacteric led to an even
worse edition of the father-substitute, thanks to which she was
cheated out of the late blossoming of her sexuality. The neurosis reveals, flickering under the repression, the eroticism of
the aging woman who still wants to please (affectation).[15]

Case 2

707   A man of thirty-four, of small build, with a clever, kindly
expression. He was easily embarrassed, blushed often. He had
come for treatment on account of "nervousness." He said he
was very irritable, readily fatigued, had nervous stomach-trou-
ble, was often so deeply depressed that he sometimes thought
of suicide.

708   Before coming to me for treatment he had sent me a circum-
stantial autobiography, or rather a history of his illness, in order
to prepare me for his visit. His story began: "My father was a
very big and strong man." This sentence awakened my curiosity;
I turned over a page and there read: "When I was fifteen a big
lad of nineteen took me into a wood and indecently assaulted
me."

709   The numerous gaps in the patient's story induced me to obtain a more exact anamnesis from him, which led to the following disclosures: The patient was the youngest of three brothers.
His father, a big, red-haired man, was formerly a soldier in the
Swiss Guard at the Vatican; later he became a policeman. He
was a stern, gruff old soldier, who brought up his sons with mili-
tary discipline; he issued commands, did not call them by name,
but whistled for them. He had spent his youth in Rome, and
during his gay life there had contracted syphilis, from the consequences of which he still suffered in old age. He was fond of
talking about his adventures in early life. His eldest son (considerably older than the patient) was exactly like him, a big,
strong man with red hair. The mother was an ailing woman,
prematurely aged. Exhausted and tired of life, she died at forty
when the patient was eight years old. He preserved a tender and
beautiful memory of his mother.

15 [Orig.: . . . but dares not acknowledge her sexuality.]

710   At school he was always the whipping-boy and always the
object of his schoolfellows' mockery. He thought his peculiar
dialect might be to blame. Later he was apprenticed to a strict
and unkind master, with whom he stuck it out for over two
years, under conditions so trying that all the other apprentices
ran away. At fifteen the assault already mentioned took place,
together with several other, milder homosexual experiences.
Then fate packed him off to France. There he made the acquaintance of a man from the south, a great boaster and Don
Juan. He dragged the patient to a brothel; he went unwillingly
and out of fear, and found he was impotent. Later he went to
Paris, where his eldest brother, a master-mason and the replica
of his father, was leading a dissolute life. The patient stayed
there a long time, badly paid and helping his sister-in-law out
of pity. The brother often took him along to a brothel, but he
was always impotent.

711   One day his brother asked him to make over to him his in-
heritance, 6,000 francs. The patient consulted his second
brother, who was also in Paris, and who urgently tried to dis-
suade him from handing over the money, because it would only
be squandered. Nevertheless the patient went and gave his in-
heritance to his brother, who naturally ran through it in the
shortest possible time. And the second brother, who would have
dissuaded him, was also let in for 500 francs. To my astonished
question why he had so light-heartedly given the money to his
brother without any guarantee he replied: well, he asked for it.
He was not a bit sorry about the money, he would give him
another 6,000 francs if he had it. The eldest brother afterwards
went to the bad altogether and his wife divorced him.

712   The patient returned to Switzerland and remained for a year
without regular employment, often suffering from hunger. During this time he made the acquaintance of a family and became
a frequent visitor. The husband belonged to some peculiar sect,
was a hypocrite, and neglected his family. The wife was elderly,
ill, and weak, and moreover pregnant. There were six children,
all living in great poverty. For this woman the patient developed
a warm affection and shared with her the little he possessed. She
told him her troubles, saying she felt sure she would die in childbed. He promised her (although he possessed nothing) that he
would take charge of the children and bring them up. The

woman did die in childbed, but the orphanage interfered and allowed him only one child. So now he had a child but no family, and naturally could not bring it up by himself. He thus came to think of marrying. But as he had never yet fallen in love with a girl he was in great perplexity.

713 It then occurred to him that his elder brother was divorced from his wife, and he resolved to marry her. He wrote to her in Paris, saying what he intended. She was seventeen years older than he, but not averse to his plan. She invited him to come to Paris to talk matters over. But on the eve of the journey fate willed that he should run an iron nail into his foot, so that he could not travel. After a while, when the wound was healed, he went to Paris and found that he had imagined his sister-in-law, now his fiancée, to be younger and prettier than she really was. The wedding took place, however, and three months later the first coitus, on his wife's initiative. He himself had no desire for it. They brought up the child together, he in the Swiss and she in the Parisian fashion, as she was a French woman. At the age of nine the child was run over and killed by a cyclist. The patient then felt very lonely and dismal at home. He proposed to his wife that they should adopt a young girl, whereupon she broke out into a fury of jealousy. Then, for the first time in his life, he fell in love with a young girl, and simultaneously the neurosis started with deep depression and nervous exhaustion, for meanwhile his life at home had become a hell.

714 My suggestion that he should separate from his wife was dismissed out of hand, on the ground that he could not take it upon himself to make the old woman unhappy on his account. He obviously preferred to go on being tormented, for the memories of his youth seemed to him more precious than any present joys.

715 This patient, too, moved all through his life in the magic circle of the family constellation. The strongest and most fateful factor was the relationship to the father; its masochistic-homosexual colouring is clearly apparent in everything he did. Even the unfortunate marriage was determined by the father, for the patient married the divorced wife of his elder brother, which amounted to marrying his mother. At the same time, his wife was the mother-substitute for the woman who died in childbed. The neurosis set in the moment the libido was withdrawn from

the infantile relationship and for the first time came a bit nearer to an individually determined goal. In this as in the previous case, the family constellation proved to be by far the stronger, so that the narrow field of neurosis was all that was left over for the struggling individuality.

Case 3

716   A 36-year-old peasant woman, of average intelligence, healthy appearance, and robust build, mother of three healthy children. Comfortable economic circumstances. She came to the clinic for the following reasons: for some weeks she had been terribly wretched and anxious, slept badly, had terrifying dreams, and also suffered by day from anxiety and depression. She stated that all these things were without foundation, she herself was surprised at them, and had to admit that her husband was quite right when he insisted that it was all "stuff and nonsense." Nevertheless, she simply could not get over them. Often strange thoughts came into her head; she was going to die and would go to hell. She got on very well with her husband.

717   Examination of the case yielded the following results. Some weeks before, she happened to take up some religious tracts which had long lain about the house unread. There she was informed that people who swore would go to hell. She took this very much to heart, and ever since then had been thinking that she must stop people swearing or she would go to hell too. About a fortnight before she read these tracts her father, who lived with her, had suddenly died of a stroke. She was not actually present at his death, but arrived only when he was already dead. Her terror and grief were very great.

718   In the days following his death she thought much about it all, wondering why her father had to die so suddenly. During these meditations she suddenly remembered that the last words she had heard her father say were: "I am one of those who have got into the devil's clutches." This memory filled her with trepidation, and she recalled how often her father had sworn savagely. She also began to wonder whether there was really a life after death, and whether her father was in heaven or hell. It was during these musings that she came across the tracts and

began to read them, until she came to the place where it said that people who swore would go to hell. Then great fear and terror fell upon her; she covered herself with reproaches, she ought to have stopped her father's swearing and deserved to be punished for her negligence. She would die and would be condemned to hell. From that hour she was filled with sorrow, grew moody, tormented her husband with her obsessive ideas, and shunned all joy and conviviality.

719   The patient's life-history was as follows: She was the youngest of five brothers and sisters and had always been her father's favourite. Her father gave her everything she wanted if he possibly could. If she wanted a new dress and her mother refused it, she could be sure her father would bring her one next time he went to town. Her mother died rather early. At twenty-four she married the man of her choice, against her father's wishes. The father flatly disapproved of her choice although he had nothing particular against the man. After the wedding she made her father come and live with them. That seemed the obvious thing, she said, since the others had never suggested having him with them. He was, as a matter of fact, a quarrelsome, foulmouthed old drunkard. Husband and father-in-law, as may easily be imagined, did not get on at all. There were endless squabbles and altercations, in spite of which the patient would always dutifully fetch drink for her father from the inn. All the same, she admitted her husband was right. He was a good, patient fellow with only one failing: he did not obey her father enough. She found that incomprehensible, and would rather have seen her husband knuckle under to her father. When all's said and done, a father is still a father. In the frequent quarrels she always took her father's part. But she had nothing to say against her husband, and he was usually right in his protests, but even so one must stand by one's father.

720   Soon it began to seem to her that she had sinned against her father by marrying against his will, and she often felt, after one of these incessant wrangles, that her love for her husband had died. And since her father's death it was impossible to love him any more, for his disobedience had usually been the cause of her father's fits of raging and swearing. At one time the quarrelling had become too much for the husband, and he induced his wife to find a room for her father elsewhere, where he lived

for two years. During this time husband and wife lived together peaceably and happily. But by degrees she began to reproach herself for letting her father live alone; in spite of everything he was her father. And in the end, despite her husband's protests, she fetched her father home again because, as she said, at bottom she loved her father better than her husband. Scarcely was the old man back in the house than the strife broke out again. And so it went on till the father's sudden death.

721   After this recital she broke into a string of lamentations: she must get a divorce from her husband, she would have done so long ago but for the children. She had committed a great wrong, a grievous sin, when she married her husband against her father's wishes. She ought to have taken the man her father wanted her to have; he, certainly, would have obeyed her father, and then everything would have been all right. Oh, she wailed, her husband was not nearly as nice as her father, she could do anything with her father, but not with her husband. Her father had given her everything she wanted. And now she wanted most of all to die, so that she could be with her father.

722   When this outburst was over, I asked curiously why she had refused the husband her father had proposed?

723   It seems that the father, a small peasant on a lean little holding, had taken on as a labourer, just at the time when his youngest daughter was born, a wretched little boy, a foundling. The boy developed in a most unpleasant fashion: he was so stupid that he could not learn to read or write, or even to speak properly. He was an absolute blockhead. As he approached manhood a series of ulcers developed on his neck, some of which opened and continually discharged pus, giving this dirty, ugly creature a truly horrible appearance. His intelligence did not grow with his years, so he stayed on as a farm-labourer without any recognized wage.

724   To this oaf the father wanted to marry his favourite daughter.

725   The girl, fortunately, had not been disposed to yield, but now she regretted it, for this idiot would unquestionably have been more obedient to her father than her good man had been.

726   Here, as in the foregoing case, it must be clearly understood that the patient was not at all feeble-minded. Both possessed normal intelligence, although the blinkers of the infantile

constellation kept them from using it. That appears with quite remarkable clearness in this patient's life-story. The father's authority is never even questioned. It makes not the least difference to her that he was a quarrelsome old drunkard, the obvious cause of all the bickering and dissension; on the contrary, her husband must bow down before this bogey, and finally our patient even comes to regret that her father did not succeed in completely destroying her life's happiness. So now she sets about destroying it herself, through her neurosis, which forces on her the wish to die so that she may go to hell—whither, be it noted, her father has already betaken himself.

727   If ever we are disposed to see some demonic power at work controlling mortal destiny, surely we can see it here in these melancholy, silent tragedies working themselves out, slowly and agonizingly, in the sick souls of our neurotics. Some, step by step, continually struggling against the unseen powers, do free themselves from the clutches of the demon who drives his unsuspecting victims from one cruel fatality to another; others rise up and win to freedom, only to be dragged back later to the old paths, caught in the noose of the neurosis. You cannot even maintain that these unhappy people are always neurotics or "degenerates." If we normal people examine our lives,[16] we too perceive how a mighty hand guides us without fail to our destiny, and not always is this hand a kindly one.[17] Often we call it the hand of God or of the devil, (thereby expressing, unconsciously but correctly, a highly important psychological fact: that the power which shapes the life of the psyche has the character of an autonomous personality. At all events it is felt as such, so that today in common speech, just as in ancient times, the source of any such destiny appears as a daemon, as a good or evil spirit.

16 [Orig.: . . . from the psychanalytic standpoint . . .]

17 "Throughout we believe ourselves to be the masters of our deeds. But reviewing our lives, and chiefly taking our misfortunes and their consequences into consideration, we often cannot account for our doing this act and omitting that, making it appear as if our steps had been guided by a power foreign to us. Therefore Shakespeare says:

'Fate show thy force: ourselves we do not owe;
What is decreed must be, and be this so!' "

—Schopenhauer, "On Apparent Design in the Fate of the Individual," *Parerga and Paralipomena* (trans. by Irvine, p. 26).

728 ⟨The personification of this source goes back in the first place to the father, for which reason Freud was of the opinion that all "divine" figures have their roots in the father-imago. It can hardly be denied that they do derive from this imago, but what we are to say about the father-imago itself is another matter. For the parental imago is possessed of a quite extraordinary power; it influences the psychic life of the child so enormously that we must ask ourselves whether we may attribute such magical power to an ordinary human being at all. Obviously he possesses it, but we are bound to ask whether it is really his property. Man "possesses" many things which he has never acquired but has inherited from his ancestors. He is not born as a *tabula rasa,* he is merely born unconscious. But he brings with him systems that are organized and ready to function in a specifically human way, and these he owes to millions of years of human development. Just as the migratory and nest-building instincts of birds were never learnt or acquired individually, man brings with him at birth the ground-plan of his nature, and not only of his individual nature but of his collective nature. These inherited systems correspond to the human situations that have existed since primeval times: youth and old age, birth and death, sons and daughters, fathers and mothers, mating, and so on. Only the individual consciousness experiences these things for the first time, but not the bodily system and the unconscious. For them they are only the habitual functioning of instincts that were preformed long ago. "You were in bygone times my wife or sister," says Goethe, clothing in words the dim feelings of many.

729 ⟨I have called this congenital and pre-existent instinctual model, or pattern of behaviour, the *archetype.* This is the imago that is charged with the dynamism we cannot attribute to an individual human being. Were this power really in our hands and subject to our will, we would be so crushed with responsibility that no one in his right senses would dare to have children. But the power of the archetype is not controlled by us; we ourselves are at its mercy to an unsuspected degree. There are many who resist its influence and its compulsion, but equally many who identify with the archetype, for instance with the *patris potestas* or with the queen ant. And because everyone is

in some degree "possessed" by his specifically human preforma-
tion, he is held fast and fascinated by it and exercises the same
influence on others without being conscious of what he is doing.
The danger is just this unconscious identity with the archetype:
not only does it exert a dominating influence on the child by
suggestion, it also causes the same unconsciousness in the child,
so that it succumbs to the influence from outside and at the
same time cannot oppose it from within. The more a father
identifies with the archetype, the more unconscious and irresponsible, indeed psychotic, both he and his child will be. In
the case we have discussed, it is almost a matter of "folie à
deux.") [18]

730   In our case, it is quite obvious what the father was doing,
and why he wanted to marry his daughter to this brutish creature: he wanted to keep her with him and make her his slave
for ever. What he did is but a crass exaggeration of what is done
by thousands of so-called respectable, educated parents, who
nevertheless pride themselves on their progressive views. The
fathers who criticize every sign of emotional independence in
their children, who fondle their daughters with ill-concealed
eroticism and tyrannize over their feelings, who keep their sons
on a leash or force them into a profession and finally into a "suitable" marriage, the mothers who even in the cradle excite their
children with unhealthy tenderness, who later make them into
slavish puppets and then at last ruin their love-life out of jealousy: they all act no differently in principle from this stupid,
boorish peasant. ⟨They do not know what they are doing, and
they do not know that by succumbing to the compulsion they
pass it on to their children and make them slaves of their parents
and of the unconscious as well. Such children will long continue
to live out the curse laid on them by their parents, even when

---

18 [*Orig.:* . . . for the power of the infantile constellation has provided highly
convincing material for the religions in the course of the millennia.

[All this is not to say that we should cast the blame for original sin upon our
parents. A sensitive child, whose sympathies are only too quick to reflect in his
psyche the excesses of his parents, bears the blame for his fate in his own character. But, as our last case shows, this is not always so, for the parents can (and
unfortunately only too often do) instil the evil into the child's soul, preying
upon his ignorance in order to make him the slave of their complexes.]

the parents are long since dead. "They know not what they do." Unconsciousness is the original sin.) [19]

Case 4

731   An eight-year-old boy, intelligent, rather delicate-looking, brought to me by his mother on account of enuresis. During the consultation the child clung all the time to his mother, a pretty, youthful woman. The marriage was a happy one, but the father was strict, and the boy (the eldest child) was rather afraid of him. The mother compensated for the father's strictness by a corresponding tenderness, to which the boy responded so much that he never got away from his mother's apron-strings. He never played with his school-fellows, never went alone into the street unless he had to go to school. He feared the boys' roughness and violence and played thoughtful games at home or helped his mother with the housework. He was extremely jealous of his father, and could not bear it when the father showed tenderness to the mother.

19 [*Orig.:* It will be asked, wherein lies the magic power of the parents to bind their children to themselves, often for the whole of their lives? The psychoanalyst knows that it is nothing but sexuality on both sides.

[We are always trying not to admit the child's sexuality. But this is only because of wilful ignorance, which happens to be very prevalent again just now.*

[I have not given any real analysis of these cases. We therefore do not know what happened to these puppets of fate when they were children. A profound insight into the living soul of a child, such as we have never had before, is given in Freud's contribution to the present semi-annual volume of the *Jahrbuch* ["Analysis of a Phobia in a Five-year-old Boy"]. If I venture, after Freud's masterly presentation, to offer another small contribution to the study of the child-psyche, it is because psychoanalytic case-histories seem to me always valuable.

[* *Orig. footnote:* This was seen at the Amsterdam Congress in 1907 [First International Congress of Psychiatry and Neurology; cf. the second paper in this vol.—EDITORS], when an eminent French savant assured us that Freud's theory was nothing but "une plaisanterie." This gentleman had evidently read neither Freud's latest writings nor mine, and knew far less about the subject than a little child. This pronouncement, so admirably grounded, met with the approbation of a well-known German professor in his report to the Congress. One can but bow before such thoroughness. At the same Congress a noted German neurologist immortalized his name with the following brilliant argument: "If in Freud's view hysteria really does rest on repressed affects, then the whole German army must be hysterical."]

732   I took the boy aside and asked him about his dreams. Very often he dreamt of a *black snake that wanted to bite his face.* Then he would cry out, and his mother had to come to him from the next room and stay by his bedside.

733   In the evening he would go quietly to bed. But when falling asleep it seemed to him that a *wicked black man with a sword or a gun was lying on his bed, a tall thin man who wanted to kill him.* The parents slept in the next room. The boy often dreamt that something dreadful was going on in there, as if there were *great black snakes or evil men who wanted to kill Mama.* Then he would cry out, and Mama came to comfort him. Every time he wet his bed he called his mother, who would then have to change the bedclothes.

734   The father was a tall thin man. Every morning he stood naked at the wash-stand in full view of the boy, to perform a thorough ablution. The boy also told me that at night he often started up from sleep at the sound of strange noises in the next room; then he was always horribly afraid that something dreadful was going on in there, a struggle of some kind, but his mother would quiet him and say it was nothing.

735   It is not difficult to see what was happening in the next room. It is equally easy to understand the boy's aim in calling out for his mother: he was jealous and was separating her from the father. He did this also in the daytime whenever he saw his father caressing her. Thus far the boy was simply the father's rival for his mother's love.

736   But now comes the fact that the snake and the wicked man threaten him as well: the same thing happens to him as happens to his mother in the next room. To that extent he identifies with his mother and thus puts himself in a similar relationship to the father. This is due to his homosexual component, which feels feminine towards the father. (The bed-wetting is in this case a substitute for sexuality. Pressure of urine in dreams and also in the waking state is often an expression of some other pressure, for instance of fear, expectation, suppressed excitement, inability to speak, the need to express an unconscious content, etc. In our case the substitute for sexuality has the significance of a premature masculinity which is meant to compensate the inferiority of the child.

737   (Although I do not intend to go into the psychology of

111

dreams in this connection, the motif of the black snake and of the black man should not pass unmentioned. Both these terrifying spectres threaten the dreamer as well as his mother. "Black" indicates something dark, the unconscious. The dream shows that the mother-child relationship is menaced by unconsciousness. The threatening agency is represented by the mythological motif of the "father animal"; in other words the father appears as threatening. This is in keeping with the tendency of the child to remain unconscious and infantile, which is decidedly dangerous. For the boy, the father is an anticipation of his own masculinity, conflicting with his wish to remain infantile. The snake's attack on the boy's face, the part that "sees," represents the danger to consciousness (blinding).⟩ [20]

738　　This little example shows what goes on in the psyche of an eight-year-old child who is over-dependent on his parents, the blame for this lying partly on the too strict father and the too tender mother. ⟨The boy's identification with his mother and fear of his father are in this individual instance an infantile neurosis, but they represent at the same time the original human situation, the clinging of primitive consciousness to the unconscious, and the compensating impulse which strives to tear consciousness away from the embrace of the darkness. Because man has a dim premonition of this original situation behind his individual experience, he has always tried to give it generally valid expression through the universal motif of the divine hero's fight with the mother dragon, whose purpose is to deliver man from the power of darkness. This myth has a "saving," i.e., therapeutic significance, since it gives adequate expression to the dynamism underlying the individual entanglement. The myth is not to be causally explained as the consequence of a personal father-complex, but should be understood teleologically, as an attempt of the unconscious itself to rescue consciousness from the danger of regression. The ideas of "salvation" are not subsequent rationalizations of a father-complex; they are, rather,

[20] [Orig.: It is not difficult to see, from the Freudian standpoint, what the bedwetting means in this case. Micturition dreams give us the clue. Here I would refer the reader to an analysis of this kind in my paper "The Analysis of Dreams" (cf. supra, pars. 82f.). Bed-wetting must be regarded as an infantile sexual substitute, and even in the dream-life of adults it is easily used as a cloak for the pressure of sexual desire.]

archetypally preformed mechanisms for the development of consciousness.⟩ 21

739 What we see enacted on the stage of world-history happens also in the individual. The child is guided by the power of the parents as by a higher destiny. But as he grows up, the struggle between his infantile attitude and his increasing consciousness begins. The parental influence, dating from the early infantile period, is repressed and sinks into the unconscious, but is not eliminated; by invisible threads it directs the apparently individual workings of the maturing mind. Like everything that has fallen into the unconscious, the infantile situation still sends up dim, premonitory feelings, feelings of being secretly guided by otherworldly influences. ⟨Normally these feelings are not referred back to the father, but to a positive or negative

21 [Orig.: The infantile attitude, it is evident, is nothing but infantile sexuality. If we now survey all the far-reaching possibilities of the infantile constellation, we are obliged to say that in essence our life's fate is identical with the fate of our sexuality. If Freud and his school devote themselves first and foremost to tracing out the individual's sexuality, it is certainly not in order to excite piquant sensations but to gain a deeper insight into the driving forces that determine the individual's fate. In this we are not saying too much, but rather understating the case. For, when we strip off the veils shrouding the problems of individual destiny, we at once widen our field of vision from the history of the individual to the history of nations. We can take a look, first of all, at the history of religion, at the history of the fantasy systems of whole peoples and epochs. The religion of the Old Testament exalted the paterfamilias into the Jehovah of the Jews, whom the people had to obey in fear and dread. The patriarchs were a stepping-stone to the Deity. The neurotic fear in Judaism, an imperfect or at any rate unsuccessful attempt at sublimation by a still too barbarous people, gave rise to the excessive severity of Mosaic law, the compulsive ceremonial of the neurotic.* Only the prophets were able to free themselves from it; for them the identifica-tion with Jehovah, complete sublimation, was successful. They became the fathers of the people. Christ, the fulfiller of their prophecies, put an end to this fear of God and taught mankind that the true relation to the Deity is love. Thus he destroyed the compulsive ceremonial of the law and was himself the exponent of the personal loving relationship to God. Later, the imperfect sublimations of the Christian Mass resulted once again in the ceremonial of the Church, from which only those of the numerous saints and reformers who were really capable of sublimation were able to break free. Not without cause, therefore, does modern theology speak of the liberating effect of "inner" or "personal" experience, for always the ardour of love transmutes fear and compulsion into a higher, freer type of feeling.

[* Orig. footnote: Cf. Freud, Zeitschrift für Religionspsychologie (1907).] [I.e., "Obsessive Acts and Religious Practices."—EDITORS.]

deity. This change is accomplished partly under the influence of education, partly spontaneously. It is universal. Also, it resists conscious criticism with the force of an instinct, for which reason the soul (*anima*) may fittingly be described as *naturaliter religiosa*. The reason for this development, indeed its very possibility, is to be found in the fact that the child possesses an inherited system that anticipates the existence of parents and their influence upon him. In other words, behind the father stands the archetype of the father, and in this pre-existent archetype lies the secret of the father's power, just as the power which forces the bird to migrate is not produced by the bird itself but derives from its ancestors.

740   It will not have escaped the reader that the role which falls to the father-imago in our case is an ambiguous one. The threat it represents has a dual aspect: fear of the father may drive the boy out of his identification with the mother, but on the other hand it is possible that his fear will make him cling still more closely to her. A typically neurotic situation then arises: he wants and yet does not want, saying yes and no at the same time.

741   This double aspect of the father-imago is characteristic of the archetype in general: it is capable of diametrically opposite effects and acts on consciousness rather as Yahweh acted towards Job—ambivalently. And, as in the Book of Job, man is left to take the consequences. We cannot say with certainty that the archetype always acts in this way, for there are experiences which prove the contrary. But they do not appear to be the rule.) [22]

742   An instructive and well-known example of the ambivalent behaviour of the father-imago is the love-episode in the Book of Tobit.[23] Sara, the daughter of Raguel, of Ecbatana, desires to marry. But her evil fate wills it that seven times, one after the

[22] [*Orig.*: These are the roots of the first religious sublimations. In the place of the father with his constellating virtues and faults there appears on the one hand an altogether sublime deity, and on the other hand the devil, who in modern times has been largely whittled away by the realization of one's own moral responsibility. Sublime love is attributed to the former, low sexuality to the latter. As soon as we enter the field of neurosis, this antithesis is stretched to the limit. God becomes the symbol of the most complete sexual repression, the devil the symbol of sexual lust. Thus it is that the conscious expression of the father-constellation, like every expression of an unconscious complex when it appears in consciousness, acquires its Janus face, its positive and its negative components.]
[23] Chs. 3 : 7ff. and 8 : 1ff.

other, she chooses a husband who dies on the wedding-night. It is the evil spirit Asmodeus, by whom she is persecuted, that kills these men. She prays to Yahweh to let her die rather than suffer this shame again, for she is despised even by her father's maid-servants. The eighth bridegroom, her cousin Tobias, the son of Tobit, is sent to her by God. He too is led into the bridal chamber. Then old Raguel, who had only pretended to go to bed, goes out and thoughtfully digs his son-in-law's grave, and in the morning sends a maid to the bridal chamber to make sure that he is dead. But this time Asmodeus' role is played out, for Tobias is alive.

743   ⟨The story shows father Raguel in his two roles, as the inconsolable father of the bride and the provident digger of his son-in-law's grave. Humanly speaking he seems beyond reproach, and it is highly probable that he was. But there is still the evil spirit Asmodeus and his presence needs explaining. If we suspect old Raguel personally of playing a double role, this malicious insinuation would apply only to his sentiments; there is no evidence that he committed murder. These wicked deeds transcend the old man's daughter-complex as well as Sara's father-complex, for which reason the legend fittingly ascribes them to a demon. Asmodeus plays the role of a jealous father who will not give up his beloved daughter and only relents when he remembers his own positive aspect, and in that capacity at last gives Sara a pleasing bridegroom. He, significantly enough, is the eighth: the last and highest stage.[24] Asmodeus stands for the negative aspect of the father archetype, for the archetype is the genius and daemon of the personal human being, "the god of human nature, changeful of countenance, white and black." [25] The legend offers a psychologically correct explanation: it does not attribute superhuman evil to Raguel, it distinguishes between man and daemon, just as psychology must distinguish between what the human individual is and can do and what must be ascribed to the congenital, instinctual system, which the individual has not made but finds within him. We would be doing the gravest injustice to Raguel if we held

24 ⟨Cf. the axiom of Maria and the discussion of 3 and 4, 7 and 8, in *Psychology and Alchemy*, pars. 201ff. and 209.⟩
25 ⟨Horace, *Epistles*, II, 2, 187–89.⟩

him responsible for the fateful power of this system, that is, of the archetype.

744   ⟨The potentialities of the archetype, for good and evil alike, transcend our human capacities many times, and a man can appropriate its power only by identifying with the daemon, by letting himself be possessed by it, thus forfeiting his own humanity. The fateful power of the father complex comes from the archetype, and this is the real reason why the *consensus gentium* puts a divine or daemonic figure in place of the father. The personal father inevitably embodies the archetype, which is what endows his figure with its fascinating power. The archetype acts as an amplifier, enhancing beyond measure the effects that proceed from the father, so far as these conform to the inherited pattern.⟩ [26]

[26] [*Orig.:* Unfortunately medical etiquette forbids me to report a case of hysteria which fits this pattern exactly, except that there were not seven husbands but only three, unluckily chosen under all the ominous signs of an infantile constellation. Our first case, too, belongs to this category, and in our third case we see the old peasant at work, preparing to dedicate his daughter to a like fate.

[As a pious and dutiful daughter (cf. her prayer in Tobit, ch. 3), Sara has brought about the usual sublimation and splitting of the father-complex, on the one hand elevating her infantile love into the worship of God, and on the other turning the obsessive power of the father into the persecuting demon Asmodeus. The story is beautifully worked out and shows father Raguel in his two roles, as the inconsolable father of the bride and the provident digger of his son-in-law's grave, whose fate he foresees.

[This pretty fable has become a classic example in my analytical work, for we frequently meet with cases where the father-demon has laid his hand upon his daughter, so that her whole life long, even when she does marry, there is never a true inward union, because her husband's image never succeeds in obliterating the unconscious and continually operative infantile father-ideal. This is true not only of daughters, but also of sons. An excellent example of this kind of father-constellation can be found in Brill's recently published "Psychological Factors in Dementia Praecox" (1908).

[In my experience it is usually the father who is the decisive and dangerous object of the child's fantasy, and if ever it happened to be the mother I was able to discover behind her a grandfather to whom she belonged in her heart.

[I must leave this question open, because my findings are not sufficient to warrant a decision. It is to be hoped that experience in the years to come will sink deeper shafts into this obscure territory, on which I have been able to shed but a fleeting light, and will discover more about the secret workshop of the demon who shapes our fate, of whom Horace says:

"Scit Genius natale comes qui temperat astrum,
Naturae deus humanae, mortalis in unum,
Quodque caput, vultu mutabilis, albus et ater."]

PSYCHIC CONFLICTS IN A CHILD

[The third of a series of lectures on "The Association Method," delivered on the 20th anniversary of the opening of Clark University, Worcester, Massachusetts, September, 1909. The original version was published under the title "Über Konflikte der kindlichen Seele," *Jahrbuch für psychoanalytische und psychopathologische Forschungen*, II (1910), 33ff. It was translated by A. A. Brill and published in the *American Journal of Psychology*, XXI (1910), in a Clark University anniversary volume (1910), and in *Collected Papers on Analytical Psychology* (1st edn., London, 1916; 2nd edn., London, 1917, and New York, 1920). The revised version, of which this present essay is a translation, appeared in *Psychologie und Erziehung* (Zurich, 1946). The first two lectures comprising "The Association Method" were never published in German but were included in the aforementioned 1910 and 1916 publications. See Vol. 2 of the *Coll. Works.*—EDITORS.]

FOREWORD TO THE SECOND EDITION

I am publishing this little study just as it is, without making any alterations for the second edition. Although in point of fact our conceptions have been considerably modified and extended since these observations first appeared in 1910, I do not feel that the subsequent modifications would justify me in describing the views put forward in the first edition as basically false, an imputation that has been laid against me in certain quarters. On the contrary, just as the observations here recorded have retained their value as facts, so also have the conceptions themselves. But no conception is ever all-embracing, for it is always dominated by a point of view. The point of view adopted in this work is psycho-biological. It is naturally not the only one possible, indeed there are several others. Thus, more in accord with the spirit of Freudian psychology, this little piece of child psychology could be regarded from the purely hedonistic standpoint, the psychological process being conceived as a movement dominated by the pleasure principle. The main motives would then be the desire for and the striving towards the most pleasurable, and hence the most satisfying, realization of fantasy. Or, following Adler's suggestion, one could regard the same material from the standpoint of the power principle, an approach which is psychologically just as legitimate as that of the hedonistic principle. Or one could employ a purely logical approach, with the intention of demonstrating the development of logical processes in the child. One could even approach the matter from the standpoint of the psychology of religion and give prominence to the earliest beginnings of the God-concept. I have been content to steer a middle course that keeps to the psychobiological method of observation, without attempting to subordinate the material to this or that hypothetical key principle. In so doing I am not, of course, contesting the legitimacy of such principles, for they are all included in our human nature; but only a very one-sided specialist would think of declaring as universally valid the heuristic principle that had proved its particular value for his discipline or for his individual method of observation. The essence of human psychology, precisely because so many different possible principles exist, can never be fully comprehended under any one of them, but only under the totality of individual aspects.

The basic hypothesis of the view advanced in this work is that sexual interest plays a not inconsiderable role in the nascent process of infantile thinking, an hypothesis that should meet with no serious opposition. A contrary hypothesis would certainly come up against too many well-observed facts, quite apart from its being extraordinarily improbable that a fundamental instinct of such cardinal importance for human psychology should not make itself felt in the infantile psyche from the very beginning.

On the other hand I also lay stress on the significance of *thinking* and the importance of concept-building for the solution of psychic conflicts. It should be sufficiently clear from what follows that the initial sexual interest strives only figuratively towards an immediate sexual goal, but far more towards the development of thinking. Were this not so, the solution of the conflict could be reached solely through the attainment of a sexual goal, and not through the mediation of an intellectual concept. But precisely the latter is the case, from which we may conclude that infantile sexuality is not to be identified outright with adult sexuality, since adult sexuality cannot be adequately replaced by concept-building, but is in most cases only satisfied with the real sexual goal, namely the tribute of normal sexual functioning which nature exacts. On the other hand, we know from experience that the infantile beginnings of sexuality can also lead to real sexual functioning—masturbation—when the conflicts are not resolved. The building of concepts, however, opens out to the libido a channel that is capable of further development, so that its continual, active realization is assured. Given a certain intensity of conflict, the absence of concept-building acts as a hindrance which thrusts the libido back into its initial sexuality, with the result that these beginnings or buddings are brought prematurely to an abnormal pitch of development. This produces an infantile neurosis. Gifted children in particular, whose mental demands begin to develop early on account of their intelligent disposition, run a serious risk of premature sexual realization through the suppression of what their parents and teachers would call an unsuitable curiosity.

As these reflections show, I do not regard the thinking function as just a makeshift function of sexuality which sees itself hindered in its pleasurable realization and is therefore compelled to pass over into the thinking function; but, while perceiving in infantile sexuality the beginnings of a future sexual function, I also discern there the seeds of higher spiritual functions. The fact that infantile conflicts can be resolved through concept-building speaks in favour of this, and also the fact that even in adult life the vestiges of infantile sexuality are the seeds of vital spiritual functions. The fact that adult sexuality grows out of this polyvalent germinal disposition does not prove that infantile sexuality is "sexuality" pure and simple. I therefore dispute the rightness of Freud's idea of the "polymorphous-perverse" disposition of the child. It is simply a *polyvalent* disposition. If we proceeded according to the Freudian formula, we should have to speak, in embryology, of the ectoderm as the brain, because from it the brain is ultimately developed. But much also develops from it besides the brain, for instance the sense organs and other things.

December, 1915   C. G. J.

FOREWORD TO THE THIRD EDITION

Since this paper first appeared, almost thirty years have gone by. Yet it would seem that this little work has not given up the ghost, but is in increasing demand with the public. In one or two respects, certainly, it has never grown stale, firstly because it presents a simple series of facts such as occur repeatedly and are found to be much the same everywhere; secondly because it demonstrates something of great practical and theoretical importance, namely the characteristic striving of the child's fantasy to outgrow its "realism" and to put a "symbolic" interpretation in the place of scientific rationalism. This striving is evidently a natural and spontaneous expression of the psyche, which for that very reason cannot be traced back to any "repression" whatsoever. I stressed this particular point in my Foreword to the second edition, and my mention of it there has not lost its topicality, since the myth of the polymorphous sexuality of the child is still sedulously believed in by the majority of specialists. The repression theory is as grossly overestimated as ever, while the natural phenomena of psychic transformation are accordingly underestimated, if not entirely ignored. In 1912, I made these phenomena the subject of a compendious study, which cannot be said even now to have penetrated the intellects of psychologists as a class. I trust therefore that the present modest and factual report will succeed in rousing the reader to reflection. Theories in psychology are the very devil. It is true that we need certain points of view for their orienting and heuristic value; but they should always be regarded as mere auxiliary concepts that can be laid aside at any time. We still know so very little about the psyche that it is positively grotesque to think we are far enough advanced to frame general theories. We have not even established the empirical extent of the psyche's phenomenology: how then can we dream of general theories? No doubt theory is the best cloak for lack of experience and ignorance, but the consequences are depressing: bigotedness, superficiality, and scientific sectarianism.

To document the polyvalent germinal disposition of the child with a sexual terminology borrowed from the stage of fully-fledged sexuality is a dubious undertaking. It means drawing everything else in the child's make-up into the orbit of sexual interpretation, so that on the one hand the concept of sexuality is blown up to fantastic proportions and becomes nebulous, while on the other hand spiritual factors are seen as warped and stunted instincts. Views of this kind lead to a rationalism which is not even remotely capable of doing justice to the essential polyvalence of the infantile disposition. Even though a child may be preoccupied with matters which, for adults, have an undoubtedly sexual complexion, this does not prove that the nature of the child's preoccupation is to be regarded as equally sexual. For the cautious and conscientious investigator sexual terminology, as applied to infantile phenomena, can be deemed at most a professional *façon de parler*. I have my qualms about its appropriateness.

Apart from a few small improvements I am allowing this paper to appear once again in unaltered form.

December, 1938   C. G. J.

PSYCHIC CONFLICTS IN A CHILD

1   About the time when Freud published his report on the case
of "Little Hans," [1] I received from a father who was acquainted
with psychoanalysis a series of observations concerning his little
daughter, then four years old.

2   These observations have so much that bears upon, and sup-
plements, Freud's report on "Little Hans" that I cannot refrain
from making this material accessible to a wider public. The
widespread incomprehension, not to say indignation, with
which "Little Hans" was greeted, was for me an additional reason for publishing my material, although it is nothing like as
extensive as that of "Little Hans." Nevertheless, it contains
points which seem to confirm how typical the case of "Little
Hans" is. So-called "scientific" criticism, so far as it has taken
any notice at all of these important matters, has once more
proved overhasty, seeing that people have still not learned first
to examine and then to judge.

3   The little girl to whose sagacity and intellectual sprightli-
ness we are indebted for the following observations is a healthy,
lively child of emotional temperament. She has never been seriously ill, nor had she ever shown any trace of "nervous" symptoms.

[1] "Analysis of a Phobia in a Five-year-old Boy," *Standard Edition of the Complete
Psychological Works of Sigmund Freud*, X (1955; first pub. 1909).

4   Livelier systematic interests awakened in the child about her third year; she began to ask questions and to spin wishful fantasies. In the report which now follows we shall, unfortunately, have to give up the idea of a consistent exposition, for it is made up of anecdotes which treat of one isolated experience out of a whole cycle of similar ones, and which cannot, therefore, be dealt with scientifically and systematically, but must rather take the form of a story. We cannot dispense with this mode of exposition in the present state of our psychology, for we are still a long way from being able in all cases to separate with unerring certainty what is curious from what is typical.

5   When the child, whom we will call Anna, was about three years old, she had the following conversation with her grandmother:

"Granny, why are your eyes so dim?"

"Because I am old."

"But you will become young again?"

"Oh dear, no. I shall become older and older, and then I shall die."

"And what then?"

"Then I shall be an angel."

"And then you will be a baby again?"

6   The child found here a welcome opportunity for the provisional solution of a problem. For some time she had been in the habit of asking her mother whether she would ever have a real live doll, a baby brother, which naturally gave rise to the question of where babies come from. As such questions were asked quite spontaneously and unobtrusively, the parents attached no significance to them, but responded to them as lightly as the child herself seemed to ask them. Thus one day she was told the pretty story that children are brought by the stork. Anna had already heard somewhere a slightly more serious version, namely that children are little angels who live in heaven and are then brought down by the said stork. This theory seems to have become the point of departure for the little one's investigating activities. From the conversation with the grandmother it could be seen that this theory was capable of wide application; for it solved in a comforting manner not only the painful thought of dying, but at the same time the riddle of where children come from. Anna seemed to be saying to herself: "When somebody

dies he becomes an angel, and then he becomes a child." Solutions of this sort, which kill at least two birds with one stone, used to be tenaciously adhered to even in science, and cannot be undone in the child's mind without a certain amount of shock. In this simple conception there lie the seeds of the reincarnation theory, which, as we know, is still alive today in millions of human beings.[2]

7   Just as the birth of a little sister was the turning point in the history of "Little Hans," so in this case it was the arrival of a baby brother, which took place when Anna had reached the age of four. The problem of where children come from, hardly touched upon so far, now became topical. The mother's pregnancy had apparently passed unnoticed; that is to say, Anna had never made any observations on this subject. On the evening before the birth, when labour pains were just beginning, the child found herself in her father's room. He took her on his knee and said, "Tell me, what would you say if you got a little brother tonight?" "I would kill him," was the prompt answer. The expression "kill" looks very alarming, but in reality it is quite harmless, for "kill" and "die" in child language only mean to "get rid of," either actively or passively, as has already been pointed out a number of times by Freud. I once had to treat a fifteen-year-old girl who, under analysis, had a recurrent association, and kept on thinking of Schiller's "Song of the Bell." She had never really read the poem, but had once glanced through it, and could only remember something about a cathedral tower. She could recall no further details. The passage goes:

> From the tower
> The bell-notes fall
> Heavy and sad
> For the funeral. . . .
>
> Alas it is the wife and mother,
> Little wife and faithful mother,
> Whom the dark prince of the shadows
> Snatches from her spouse's arms. . . .

2 [In the light of Professor Jung's later researches these theories can be understood as based upon the archetype of rebirth, in the unconscious. Several other examples of archetypal activity are to be found in this essay.—EDITORS.]

8   She naturally loved her mother dearly and had no thought of her death, but on the other hand the present position was this: she had to go away with her mother for five weeks, staying with relatives; the year before, the mother had gone by herself, and the daughter (an only and spoilt child) was left at home alone with her father. Unfortunately this year it was the "little wife" who was being snatched from the arms of her spouse, whereas the daughter would greatly have preferred the "faithful mother" to be parted from her child.

9   On the lips of a child, therefore, "kill" is a perfectly harmless expression, especially when one knows that Anna used it quite promiscuously for all possible kinds of destruction, removal, demolition, etc. All the same this tendency is worth noting. (Compare the analysis of "Little Hans.")

10   The birth occurred in the early morning. When all traces of the birth had been removed, together with the bloodstains, the father went into the room where Anna slept. She awoke as he entered. He told her the news of the arrival of a little brother, which she took with a surprised and tense expression on her face. The father then picked her up and carried her into the bedroom. Anna threw a rapid glance at her rather wan-looking mother and then displayed something like a mixture of embarrassment and suspicion, as if thinking, "What's going to happen now?" She evinced hardly any pleasure at the sight of the new arrival, so that the cool reception she gave it caused general disappointment. For the rest of the morning she kept very noticeably away from her mother; this was the more striking, as normally she was always hanging around her. But once, when her mother was alone, she ran into the room, flung her arms round her neck and whispered hurriedly, "Aren't you going to die now?"

11   Something of the conflict in the child's soul is now revealed to us. The stork theory had obviously never caught on properly, but the fruitful rebirth hypothesis undoubtedly had, according to which a person helps a child into life by dying. Mama ought therefore to die. Why, then, should Anna feel any pleasure over the new arrival, of whom she was beginning to feel childishly jealous anyway? Hence, she had to assure herself at a favourable opportunity whether Mama was going to die or not. Mama did not die. With this happy issue, however, the rebirth theory re-

ceived a severe setback. How was it now possible to explain little brother's birth and the origins of children in general? There still remained the stork theory, which, though never expressly rejected, had been implicitly waived in favour of the rebirth hypothesis.[3] The next attempts at explanation unfortunately remained hidden from the parents, as the child went to stay with her grandmother for a few weeks. From the latter's report, however, it appears that the stork theory was much discussed, there being of course a tacit agreement to support it.

12   When Anna returned home she again displayed, on meeting her mother, the same mixture of embarrassment and suspicion as after the birth. The impression was quite explicit to both parents, though not explicable. Her behaviour towards the baby was very nice. Meantime a nurse had arrived, who made a deep impression on little Anna with her uniform—an extremely negative impression at first, as she evinced the greatest hostility towards her in all things. Thus nothing would induce her to let herself be undressed in the evenings and put to bed by this nurse. The reason for this resistance soon became clear in a stormy scene by the bedside of the little brother, when Anna shouted at the nurse, "That's not your little brother, he is mine!" Gradually, however, she became reconciled to the nurse and began to play nurse herself; she had to have her white cap and apron, nursing her little brother and her dolls in turn. In contrast to her former mood the present one was unmistakably elegiac and dreamy. She often sat for hours crouched under the table singing long stories to herself and making rhymes, partly incomprehensible, but consisting partly of wishful fantasies on

[3] One might ask at this point why one is justified in supposing at all that children of this age worry their heads about such theories. The answer is that children are intensely interested in all the sensuously perceptible things going on around them. This also shows itself in the well-known endless questions concerning the why and wherefore of everything. One has to put off the dun-coloured spectacles of our culture for a moment if one wants to understand the psychology of a child. For everybody the birth of a child is quite the most important event there can possibly be. For our civilized thinking, however, birth has lost much of its biological uniqueness, just as sex has done. But somewhere or other the mind must have stored up the correct biological valuations impressed upon it all through the ages. What could be more probable than that the child still has these valuations and makes no bones about showing them, before civilization spreads like a pall over his primitive thinking?

the "nurse" theme ("I am a nurse of the green cross"), and partly of distinctly painful feelings which were struggling for expression.

13   Here we meet with an important new feature in the little one's life: reveries, the first stirrings of poetry, moods of an elegiac strain—all of them things which are usually to be met with only at a later phase of life, at a time when the youth or maiden is preparing to sever the family tie, to step forth into life as an independent person, but is still inwardly held back by aching feelings of homesickness for the warmth of the family hearth. At such a time they begin weaving poetic fancies in order to compensate for what is lacking. To approximate the psychology of a four-year-old to that of the boy or girl approaching puberty may at first sight seem paradoxical; the affinity lies, however, not in the age but in the mechanism. The elegiac reveries express the fact that part of the love which formerly belonged, and should belong, to a real object, is now *introverted,* that is, it is turned inwards into the subject and there produces an increased fantasy activity.[4] Whence comes this introversion? Is it a psychological manifestation peculiar to this period, or does it come from a conflict?

14   On this point the following episode is enlightening. Anna disobeyed her mother more and more often, saying insolently, "I shall go back to Granny!"

"But I shall be sad if you leave me."

"Ah, but you've got baby brother."

15   The mother's reaction shows us what the child was really getting at with her threats to go away again: she obviously wanted to hear what her mother would say to her proposal, what her attitude was in general, and whether the little brother had not ousted her altogether from her mother's affection. One must

---

4 This process is altogether typical. When life comes up against an obstacle, so that no adaptation can be achieved and the transference of libido to reality is suspended, then an introversion takes place. That is to say, instead of the libido working towards reality there is an increased fantasy activity which aims at removing the obstacle, or at least removing it in fantasy, and this may in time lead to a practical solution. Hence the exaggerated sexual fantasies of neurotics, who in this way try to overcome their specific repression; hence also the typical fantasy of stammerers, that they really possess a great talent for eloquence. (That they have some claims in this respect is brought home to us by Alfred Adler's thoughtful studies on organ inferiority.)

not, however, fall for this transparent piece of trickery. The child could see and feel perfectly well that she was not stinted of anything essential in her mother's love, despite the existence of her baby brother. The veiled reproach she levels at her mother on that score is therefore unjustified, and to the trained ear this is betrayed by the slightly affected tone of voice. One often hears similar tones even with grown-up people. Such a tone, which is quite unmistakable, does not expect to be taken seriously and obtrudes itself all the more forcibly for that reason. Nor should the reproach be taken to heart by the mother, for it is merely the forerunner of other and this time more serious resistances. Not long after the conversation narrated above, the following scene took place:

Mother: "Come, we'll go into the garden."

Anna: "You're lying to me. Watch out if you're not telling the truth!"

Mother: "What are you thinking of? Of course I'm telling the truth."

Anna: "No, you are not telling the truth."

Mother: "You'll soon see whether I'm telling the truth: we are going into the garden this minute."

Anna: "Is that true? You're quite sure it's true? You're not lying?"

16   Scenes of this kind were repeated a number of times. But this time the tone was more vehement and insistent, and also the accent on the word "lie" betrayed something special which the parents did not understand; indeed they attributed far too little significance at first to the child's spontaneous utterances. In this they were only doing what all official education does. We do not usually listen to children at any stage of their careers; in all the essentials we treat them as *non compos mentis* and in all the unessentials they are drilled to the perfection of automatons. Behind resistances there always lies a question, a conflict, of which we hear soon enough at another time and on another occasion. But usually we forget to connect the thing heard with the resistances. Thus, on another occasion, Anna faced her mother with the awkward questions:

"I want to be a nurse when I grow up."

"That's what I wanted to be when I was a child."

"Why aren't you a nurse, then?"

"Well, because I am a mother instead, and so I have children of my own to nurse."

Anna (thoughtfully): "Shall I be a different woman from you? Shall I live in a different place? Shall I still talk with you?"

17   The mother's answer again shows where the child's question was leading.[5] Anna would obviously like to have a child to nurse, just as the nurse has. Where the nurse got the child from is quite clear, and Anna could get a child in the same way when she grew up. Why then wasn't Mama such a nurse—that is, how did she get the child if she didn't get it in the same way as the nurse? Anna could get a child just as the nurse had done, but how all that was going to be different in the future, or rather how she was going to be like her mother in the matter of getting children, was not so easy to see. Hence the thoughtful question "Shall I be a different woman from you?" Shall I be different in every way? The stork theory is evidently no good, the dying theory no less so, therefore one gets a child as the nurse, for example, got hers. In this natural way she, too, could get one; but how about the mother, who is no nurse and yet has children? Looking at the matter from this angle, Anna asks, "Why aren't you a nurse?"—meaning: why haven't you got your child in the plain, straightforward, natural way? This strangely indirect mode of interrogation is typical and may be connected with the child's hazy grasp of the problem, unless we are to assume a certain "diplomatic vagueness" prompted by a desire to evade direct questioning. Later we shall find evidence of this possibility.

18   Anna is therefore confronted with the question "Where does the child come from?" The stork did not bring it; Mama did not die; nor did Mama get it in the same way as the nurse. She has,

---

[5] The somewhat paradoxical view that the aim of the child's question is to be sought in the mother's answer requires a little discussion. It is one of the greatest of Freud's services to psychology that he opened up again the whole questionableness of *conscious* motives. One consequence of repressing the instincts is that the importance of conscious thinking for action is boundlessly overestimated. According to Freud, the criterion for the psychology of the act is not the conscious motive, but the *result* of the act (the result being evaluated not physically but psychologically). This view sets the act in a new and biologically revealing light. I refrain from examples and shall content myself with observing that this view is extremely valuable for psychoanalysis both in principle and as regards interpretation.

however, asked this question before and was informed by her father that the stork brings children; but this is definitely not so, she has never been deceived on this point. Therefore Papa and Mama and all the others lie. This readily explains her mistrustful attitude at the birth and the reproaches levelled against her mother. But it also explains another point, namely the elegiac reveries which we have attributed to a partial introversion. We now know the real object from which love had to be withdrawn and introverted for lack of an aim: it was withdrawn from the parents who deceived her and refused to tell her the truth. (What can this be which must not be uttered? What goes on here? Such are the parenthetic questions which the child later formulated to herself. Answer: It must be something that needs hushing up, perhaps something dangerous.) Attempts to make the mother talk and to draw out the truth by means of artful questions were futile, so resistance meets with resistance and the introversion of love begins. Naturally the capacity for sublimation in a four-year-old child is still too meagrely developed for it to render more than symptomatic service; hence she has to rely on another compensation, that is, she resorts to one of the already abandoned infantile devices for securing love by force, preferably that of crying and calling the mother at night. This had been diligently practised and exploited during her first year. It now returns and, in keeping with her age, has become well motivated and equipped with recent impressions.

19   We should mention that the Messina earthquake had just occurred, and this event was much discussed at table. Anna was extraordinarily interested in everything to do with it, getting her grandmother to tell her over and over again how the earth shook and the houses tumbled down and how many people lost their lives. That was the beginning of her nocturnal fears; she could not be left alone, her mother had to go to her and stay with her, otherwise she was afraid that the earthquake would come and the house fall in and kill her. By day, too, she was intensely occupied with such thoughts; when out walking with her mother she would pester her with such questions as "Will the house be standing when we get home? Will Papa still be alive? Are you sure there's no earthquake at home?" At every stone in the road she would ask whether it was from the earthquake. A house under construction was a house destroyed by the

earthquake, and so on. Finally she used to cry out at night that the earthquake was coming, she could hear it rumbling. Every evening she had to be solemnly promised that no earthquake would come. Various ways of calming her were tried, for instance she was told that earthquakes only occur where there are volcanoes. But then she had to be satisfied that the mountains surrounding the town were not volcanoes. This reasoning gradually led the child to an intense and, at her age, unnatural craving for knowledge, until finally all the geological pictures and atlases had to be fetched from her father's library. For hours she would rummage through them looking for pictures of volcanoes and earthquakes, and asking endless questions.

20   We see here an energetic attempt being made to sublimate fear into a desire for knowledge, which strikes us as decidedly premature at this age. But how many gifted children, suffering from exactly the same problem, do we not see being spoon-fed on this untimely sublimation, and by no means to their advantage. For if one fosters sublimation at this age one is only strengthening a neurosis. The root of the child's desire for knowledge is fear, and the fear is the expression of converted libido, that is, of an introversion that has become neurotic and is neither necessary nor favourable to the development of the child at this age. Where this desire for knowledge is ultimately leading is made clear by a series of questions which arose almost daily: "Why is Sophie [a younger sister] younger than I? Where was Freddie [her little brother] before? Was he in heaven and what was he doing there? Why did he only come down now, why not before?"

21   Such being the state of affairs, the father decided that the mother ought to tell the child the truth about her little brother at the first favourable opportunity.

22   This presented itself when, soon afterwards, Anna again inquired about the stork. Her mother told her that the story of the stork was not true, but that Freddie grew inside his mother as the flower grows out of the earth. At first he was very little, and then he grew bigger and bigger like a plant. The child listened attentively without the least surprise and then asked:
"But did he come all by himself?"
"Yes."
"But he can't walk yet!"

Sophie: "Then he crawled out."

Anna (overhearing Sophie's remark): "Is there a hole here" —pointing to her chest—"or did he come out of the mouth? Who came out of the nurse?"

²³ At this point she interrupted herself and exclaimed, "No, I know the stork brought him down from heaven!" Then, before the mother could answer her questions, she dropped the subject and again asked to see pictures of volcanoes. The evening following this conversation was calm. The sudden explanation had evidently produced in the child a whole chain of ideas, which announced themselves in a spate of questions. New and unexpected vistas were opened, and she rapidly approached the main problem: "Where did the baby come out? Was it from a hole in the chest or from the mouth?" Both suppositions qualify as acceptable theories. We even meet with young married women who still entertain the theory of the hole in the abdominal wall or of Caesarean section; this is supposed to betray a very unusual degree of innocence. As a matter of fact it is not innocence; in such cases we are practically always dealing with infantile sexual activities which in later life have brought the *vias naturales* into ill repute.

²³ᵃ It may be asked where the child got the absurd idea that there is a hole in the chest, or that the birth takes place through the mouth. Why did she not pick on one of the natural openings in the pelvis, from which things come out daily? The explanation is simple. It was not so very long since our little one had challenged all the educative arts of her mother by her heightened interest in both these openings and their remarkable products—an interest not always in accord with the demands of cleanliness and decorum. Then for the first time she became acquainted with the exceptional laws relating to these bodily regions and, being a sensitive child, she soon noticed that there was something taboo about them. Consequently this region had to be left out of her calculations, a trivial error of thought which may be forgiven in a child when one considers all those people who, despite the most powerful spectacles, can never see anything sexual anywhere. In this matter Anna reacted far more docilely than her little sister, whose scatological interests and achievements were certainly phenomenal and who even misbehaved in that way at table. She invariably described her excesses

as "funny," but Mama said no, it was not funny, and forbade such fun. The child seemed to take these incomprehensible educational sallies in good part, but she soon had her revenge. Once when a new dish appeared on the table she categorically refused to have anything to do with it, remarking that it was "not funny." Thereafter all culinary novelties were declined on the ground that they were "not funny."

24   The psychology of this negativism is quite typical and is not hard to fathom. The logic of feeling says simply: "If you don't find my little tricks funny and make me give them up, then I won't find your tricks funny either, and won't play with you." Like all childish compensations of this kind, this works on the important infantile principle "It serves you right when I'm hurt."

25   After this digression, let us return to our theme. Anna had merely shown herself docile and had so adjusted herself to the cultural demands that she thought (or at least spoke) of the simplest things last. The incorrect theories that have been substituted for the correct ones sometimes persist for years, until brusque enlightenment comes from without. It is therefore no wonder that such theories, the formation of and adherence to which is favoured even by parents and educationists, should later become determinants of important symptoms in a neurosis, or of delusions in a psychosis, as I have shown in my "Psychology of Dementia Praecox." [6] Things that have existed in the psyche for years always remain somewhere, even though they may be hidden under compensations of a seemingly different nature.

26   But even before the question is settled as to where the child actually comes out a new problem obtrudes itself: children come out of Mama, but how about the nurse? Did someone come out of her too? Then follows the abrupt exclamation, "No, I know the stork brought him down from heaven!" What is there so peculiar about the fact that nobody came out of the nurse? We recall that Anna has identified herself with the nurse and plans to become a nurse later, for she too would like to have a child, and she could get one just as easily as the nurse had

6 [In Coll. Works, Vol. 3: The Psychogenesis of Mental Disease. For the complete contents of the Collected Works of C. G. Jung, see the list at the end of this volume.—EDITORS.]

done. But now, when it is known that little brother grew in Mama, what is to be done?

27   This disquieting question is averted by a quick return to the stork-angel theory, which had never really been believed and which after a few trials is definitely abandoned. Two questions, however, remain in the air. The first is: where does the child come out? and the second, a considerably more difficult one: how is it that Mama has children while the nurse and the servants do not? Neither question is asked for the time being.

28   The next day at lunch, Anna announced, apparently out of the blue, "My brother is in Italy and has a house made of cloth and glass and it doesn't fall down."

29   Here as always it was impossible to ask for an explanation; the resistances were too great, and Anna would not have let herself be pinned down. This unique and rather officious announcement is very significant. For some three months the children had been spinning a stereotyped fantasy of a "big brother" who knew everything, could do everything, and had everything. He had been to all the places where they had not been, was allowed to do all the things they were not allowed to do, was the owner of enormous cows, horses, sheep, dogs, etc.[7] Each of them had such a big brother. The source of this fantasy is not far to seek: its model is the father, who seems to be rather like a brother to Mama. So the children too must have an equally powerful brother. This brother is very brave, he is at present in dangerous Italy and lives in an impossibly fragile house which does not fall down. For the child this is an important wish-fulfilment: the earthquake is no longer dangerous. In consequence the fear and anxiety were banished and did not return. The fear of earthquakes now entirely disappeared. Instead of calling her father to her bedside every evening to conjure away the fear, she now became more affectionate and begged him to kiss her good night. In order to test this new state of affairs, the father showed her more pictures of volcanoes and earthquakes, but Anna remained indifferent and examined the pictures coldly: "Dead people! I've seen all that before." Even the photograph of a volcanic eruption no longer held any attractions for her. Thus all her scientific interest collapsed and vanished as sud-

[7] This is a primitive definition of God.

denly as it had come. However, during the days that followed her enlightenment Anna had more important matters to attend to, for she had her newly found knowledge to disseminate among her circle of acquaintances. She began by recounting, at great length, how Freddie had grown in Mama, and herself and her younger sister likewise; how Papa grew in *his* mother and Mama in *her* mother, and the servants in their respective mothers. By dint of numerous questions she also tested whether her knowledge was firmly founded in truth, for her suspicions had been aroused in no small degree, so that repeated corroboration was needed to dissipate all her misgivings. In between times the children brought up the stork-angel theory again, but in a less believing tone, and even lectured the dolls in a singsong voice.

30   The new knowledge, however, obviously held its ground, for the phobia did not return.

31   Only once did her certainty threaten to go to pieces. About a week after the enlightenment her father had to spend the morning in bed with an attack of influenza. The children knew nothing of this, and Anna, coming into her parents' bedroom, saw the unexpected sight of her father lying in bed. She made an oddly surprised face, remained standing far away from the bed, and would not come nearer, evidently feeling shy and mistrustful again. Suddenly she burst out with the question "Why are you in bed? Have you got a plant in your inside too?"

32   Naturally her father had to laugh, and assured her that children never grew in their fathers, that as a matter of fact men did not have children, but only women, whereupon the child instantly became friendly again. But though the surface was calm the problems went on working in the depths. A few days later Anna again announced at lunch, "I had a dream last night about Noah's Ark." The father then asked her what she had dreamed, to which Anna only let out a stream of nonsense. In such cases one must simply wait and pay attention. Sure enough, after a few minutes Anna said to her grandmother, "I had a dream last night about Noah's Ark and there were lots of little animals in it." Another pause. Then she began the story for the third time: *"I had a dream last night about Noah's Ark and there were lots of little animals in it and underneath there was a lid which opened and all the little animals fell out."* Knowledge-

able persons will understand the fantasy. The children really did have a Noah's Ark, but the opening, a lid, was in the roof and not underneath. This is a delicate hint that the story about children being born from the mouth or chest was wrong, and that she had a pretty good idea of where they did come out—namely, from underneath.

33 Several weeks now passed without any noteworthy occurrences. There was one dream: *"I dreamt about Papa and Mama, they were sitting up late in the study and we children were there too."*

34 On the face of it this is just the well-known wish of children to be allowed to stay up as long as the parents. This wish is here realized, or rather it is used to mask a much more important wish, the wish to be present in the evenings when the parents are alone, and—naturally and innocently enough—in the *study* where she had seen all those interesting books and had satisfied her thirst for knowledge. In other words, she was really seeking an answer to the burning question of where little brother came from. If the children were there they would find out.

35 A few days later Anna had a nightmare, from which she awoke screaming, "The earthquake is coming, the house is beginning to shake!" Her mother went to her and comforted her, saying that there was no earthquake, everything was quiet and everybody was asleep. Then Anna said in an urgent tone, "I'd just like to see the spring, how all the little flowers come out and how all the fields are full of flowers; I want to see Freddie, he has such a dear little face. What is Papa doing—what did he say?" Her mother told her he was asleep and hadn't said anything. Anna then remarked, with a sarcastic smile, "He will probably be sick again in the morning!"

36 This text must be read backwards. The last sentence is not intended seriously, as it was uttered in a sarcastic tone of voice. The last time father was sick Anna suspected him of having "a plant in his inside." The sarcasm therefore means "He will probably have a child in the morning!" But this is not intended seriously, for Papa cannot have a child, only Mama has children; perhaps she will have another tomorrow, but where from? "What is Papa doing?" Here we have an unmistakable formulation of the difficult problem: what does Papa do if he does not produce children? Anna would very much like to find the clue

to all her problems; she would like to know how Freddie came into the world, she would like to see how the flowers come out of the earth in the spring, and these wishes all hide behind her fear of earthquakes.

37   After this intermezzo Anna slept peacefully until morning. In the morning her mother asked her what was the matter with her last night. Anna had forgotten everything and thought she had only had a dream: *"I dreamt I could make the summer and then someone threw a golliwog down the toilet."*

38   This singular dream is made up of two different scenes, which are separated by the word "then." The second part derives its material from a recent wish to have a golliwog, i.e., to have a masculine doll just as Mama has a little boy. Someone throws the golliwog down the toilet—but usually one lets quite other things drop down the toilet. The inference is that children come out just like the things into the toilet. Here we have an analogy to the *Lumpf*-theory of Little Hans. Whenever several scenes are found in one dream, each scene ordinarily represents a special variation of the working out of the complex. Thus the first part is only a variation of the theme found in the second part. We have noted above what is meant by "seeing the spring" or "seeing the flowers come out." Anna now dreams that she *can make the summer,* i.e., can cause the flowers to come out; she herself can make a little child, and the second part of the dream represents this as analogous to the making of a motion. Here we put our finger on the egoistic wish which lies behind the seemingly objective interest of the previous night's conversation.

39   A few days later the mother received a visit from a lady who was looking forward to her confinement. The children apparently noticed nothing. But the next day they amused themselves, under the guidance of the elder girl, by taking all the old newspapers out of their father's waste-paper basket and stuffing them under their frocks in front, so that the imitation was unmistakable. That night Anna again had a dream: *"I dreamt about a lady in the town, she had a very fat stomach."* As the chief actor in a dream is always the dreamer himself under a definite aspect, the game of the day before finds complete interpretation.

40   Not long after, Anna surprised her mother with the following performance: she stuck her doll under her clothes and slowly pulled it out head downwards, saying, "Look, the baby is com-

ing out, now it is all out." Anna was telling her mother: thus I conceive the problem of birth. What do you think of it? is it right? The game is really meant as a question, for, as we shall see later, this conception still had to be officially confirmed.

41   Rumination on the problem by no means ended here, as is apparent from the ideas Anna conceived during the following weeks. Thus she repeated the same game a few days later with her Teddy bear, which had the function of a specially beloved doll. Another day, pointing to a rose, she said to her grandmother, "Look, the rose is getting a baby." As the grandmother did not quite take her meaning, the child pointed to the swollen calyx: "Don't you see, it's all fat here!"

42   One day she was quarrelling with her younger sister, when the latter exclaimed angrily, "I'll kill you!" Whereupon Anna replied, "When I am dead you will be all alone, and then you'll have to pray to God for a live baby." And immediately the scene changed: Anna was the angel, and the younger sister had to kneel down before her and beg her to send a living child. In this way Anna became the child-giving mother.

43   Once they had oranges for supper. Anna impatiently asked for one and said, "I'll take an orange and I'll swallow it all down into my stomach, and then I shall get a baby."

44   This instantly reminds us of the fairytales in which childless women finally make themselves pregnant by swallowing fruit, fish and the like.[8] Anna was here trying to solve the problem of how children actually get into the mother. In so doing she takes up a position of inquiry which had never been formulated before so precisely. The solution follows in the form of an analogy, which is characteristic of the archaic thinking of the child. (Thinking in analogies is also found in the adult, in the stratum lying immediately below consciousness. Dreams bring the analogies to the surface, as also does dementia praecox.) In German and numerous other foreign fairytales one frequently finds such childish comparisons. Fairytales seem to be the myths of childhood and they therefore contain among other things the mythology which children weave for themselves concerning sexual processes. The poetry of fairytale, whose magic is felt even by the

[8] Cf. Franz Riklin, *Wishfulfillment and Symbolism in Fairy Tales* (trans. by W. A. White, Nervous and Mental Disease Monograph Series, No. 21, New York, 1915).

adult, rests not least upon the fact that some of the old theories are still alive in our unconscious. We experience a strange and mysterious feeling whenever a fragment of our remotest youth stirs into life again, not actually reaching consciousness, but merely shedding a reflection of its emotional intensity on the conscious mind.

45   The problem of how the child gets into the mother is a difficult one to solve. As the only way of getting things into the body is through the mouth, it stands to reason that the mother ate something like a fruit, which then grew inside her. But here another difficulty presents itself: one knows what comes out of the mother, but what is the use of the father? Now, it is an old rule of the mental economy to connect two unknowns and to use one to solve the other.

46   Hence the conviction rapidly fastened on the child that the father is somehow involved in the whole business, particularly in view of the fact that the problem of where children come from still leaves the question open of how they get into the mother.

47   What does the father do? This question occupied Anna to the exclusion of all else. One morning she ran into her parents' bedroom while they were still dressing, jumped into her father's bed, lay flat on her face, and flailed with her legs, crying out, "Look, is that what Papa does?" Her parents laughed and did not answer, as it only dawned on them afterwards what this performance probably signified. The analogy with the horse of Little Hans, which made such a commotion with its legs, is surprisingly close.

48   Here, with this latest achievement, the matter seemed to rest; at any rate the parents found no opportunity to make any pertinent observations. That the problem should come to a standstill at this point is not really surprising, for this is the most difficult part. The child knows nothing about sperms and nothing about coitus. There is but one possibility: the mother must eat something, for only in that way can anything get into the body. But what does the father do? The frequent comparisons with the nurse and other unmarried people were obviously to some purpose. Anna was bound to conclude that the existence of the father was in some way significant. But what on earth does he

141

do? Anna and Little Hans are agreed that it must have something to do with the legs.

49   This standstill lasted about five months, during which time no phobias or any other signs of a working through of the complex appeared. Then came the first premonition of future events. Anna's family were at that time living in a country house near a lake, where the children could bathe with their mother. As Anna was afraid to go more than knee-deep into the water, her father once took her right in with him, which led to a great outburst of crying. That evening, when going to bed, Anna said to her mother, "Papa wanted to drown me, didn't he?"

50   A few days later there was another outburst. She had continued to stand in the gardener's way until finally, for a joke, he picked her up and put her in a hole he had just dug. Anna started to cry miserably, and declared afterwards that the man had tried to bury her.

51   The upshot was that Anna woke up one night with fearful screams. Her mother went to her in the adjoining room and quieted her. Anna had dreamed that *"a train went by overhead and fell down."*

52   Here we have a parallel to the "stage coach" story of Little Hans. These incidents show clearly enough that fear was again in the air, i.e., that there was some obstacle preventing the transference of love to the parents and that therefore a large part of it was converted into fear. This time the mistrust was directed not against the mother, but against the father, who she was sure must know the secret, but would never let anything out. What could the father be doing or keeping up his sleeve? To the child this secret appeared to be something very dangerous, so obviously she felt that the worst might be expected of the father. (This childish fear of the father is to be seen particularly clearly in adults in cases of dementia praecox, which takes the lid off many unconscious processes as though it were acting on psychoanalytical principles.) Hence Anna arrived at the apparently nonsensical notion that her father wanted to drown her.

53   Meanwhile Anna had grown a little older and her interest in her father took on a special tinge which is rather hard to describe. Language has no words for the peculiar kind of tender curiosity that shone in the child's eyes.

54   It is probably no accident that the children began playing a

pretty game about this time. They called the two biggest dolls their "grandmothers" and played at hospital with them, a tool-shed being taken over as a hospital. There the grandmothers were brought, interned, and left to sit overnight. "Grand-mother" in this connection is distinctly reminiscent of the "big brother" earlier. It seems very likely that the "grandmother" deputizes for the mother. So the children were already conspiring to get the mother out of the way.[9] This intention was assisted by the fact that the mother had again given Anna cause for displeasure.

55 It came about in the following way: The gardener had laid out a large bed which he was sowing with grass. Anna helped him in this work with much pleasure, apparently without guessing the profound significance of her childish play. About a fortnight later she began to observe with delight the young grass sprouting. On one of these occasions she went to her mother and asked, "How did the eyes grow into the head?"

56 Her mother told her she didn't know. But Anna went on to ask whether God knew, or her father, and why God and her father knew everything? The mother then referred her to her father, who might be able to tell her how the eyes grew into the head. Some days later there was a family gathering at tea. After the meal had broken up, the father remained at the table reading the paper, and Anna also stayed behind. Suddenly approaching her father she said, "Tell me, how did the eyes grow into the head?"

Father: "They did not grow into the head; they were there from the beginning and grew with the head."

Anna: "Weren't the eyes planted?"

Father: "No, they just grew in the head like the nose."

Anna: "But did the mouth and the ears grow like that? And the hair?"

Father: "Yes, they all grew the same way."

9 This tendency to get rid of the mother also showed itself in the following inci-dent: The children had requisitioned the tool-shed as a house for themselves and their dolls. An important room in any house is, as we know, the toilet, which obviously cannot be lacking. Accordingly, the children went to the toilet in a corner of the tool-shed. Their mother naturally could not help spoiling this illu-sion by forbidding such games. Soon afterwards she caught the remark, "When Mama is dead we'll do it every day in the tool-shed and put on Sunday clothes every day."

Anna: "Even the hair? But the baby mice come into the world all naked. Where was the hair before? Aren't there little seeds for it?"

Father: "No. The hair, you see, comes out of little granules which are like seeds, but they are already in the skin and nobody sowed them there."

57   The father was now getting into a fix. He guessed where the little one was leading him, therefore he did not want to upset, on account of a single false application, the diplomatically introduced seed theory which she had most fortunately picked up from nature; for the child spoke with an unwonted earnestness which compelled consideration.

58   Anna (visibly disappointed, and in a distressed voice): "But how did Freddie get into Mama? Who stuck him in? And who stuck you into your mama? Where did he come out?"

59   From this sudden storm of questions the father chose the last for his first answer:

"Think, now, you know that Freddie is a boy; boys grow into men and girls into women, and only women can have children. Now, just think, where could Freddie have come out?"

Anna (laughing joyfully and pointing to her genitals): "Did he come out here?"

Father: "But of course. Surely you must have thought of that before?"

Anna (overlooking the question): "But how did Freddie get into Mama? Did anybody plant him? Was the seed sown?"

60   This extremely precise question could no longer be evaded by the father. He explained to the child, who listened with the greatest attention, that the mother is like the soil and the father like the gardener; that the father provides the seed which grows in the mother and thus produces a baby. This answer gave her extraordinary satisfaction; she immediately ran to her mother and said, "Papa has told me everything, now I know it all." But what it was she knew, she never told to anyone.

61   The new knowledge was, however, put into practice the following day. Anna went up to her mother and said brightly: "Just think, Mama, Papa told me that Freddie was a little angel and was brought down from heaven by the stork." Her mother was naturally astounded, and said, "I am quite certain your

father never told you anything of the sort." Whereupon the little one skipped away laughing.

62   This was her revenge. Her mother evidently would not or could not tell her how the eyes grew into the head; she didn't even know how Freddie had got into her. Therefore she could easily be led up the garden path with that old story about the stork. She might believe it still.

*   *   *

63   The child was now satisfied, for her knowledge had been enriched and a difficult problem solved. An even greater advantage, however, was the fact that she had won a more intimate relationship with her father, which did not prejudice her intellectual independence in the least. The father of course was left with an uneasy feeling, for he was not altogether happy about having passed on to a four-and-a-half-year-old child a secret which other parents carefully guard. He was disquieted by the thought of what Anna might do with her knowledge. What if she was indiscreet and exploited it? She might so easily instruct her playmates or gleefully play the *enfant terrible* with grown-ups. But these fears proved to be groundless. Anna never breathed a word about it, either then or at any time. The enlightenment had, moreover, brought a complete silencing of the problem, so that no more questions presented themselves. Yet the unconscious did not lose sight of the riddle of human creation. A few weeks after her enlightenment Anna recounted the following dream: She was *"in the garden and several gardeners stood making wee-wee against the trees, and Papa was also doing it."*

64   This recalls the earlier unsolved problem: what does the father do?

65   Also about this time a carpenter came into the house in order to repair an ill-fitting cupboard; Anna stood by and watched him planing the wood. That night she dreamt that the carpenter "planed off" her genitals.

66   The dream could be interpreted to mean that Anna was asking herself: will it work with me? oughtn't one to do something like what the carpenter did, in order to make it work? Such an hypothesis would indicate that this problem is particularly active in the unconscious at the moment, because there is

something not quite clear about it. That this is so was shown by the next incident, which did not, however, occur until several months later, when Anna was approaching her fifth birthday. Meantime the younger sister, Sophie, was taking a growing interest in these matters. She had been present when Anna received enlightenment at the time of the earthquake phobia, and had even thrown in an apparently understanding remark on that occasion, as the reader may remember. But in actual fact the explanation was not understood by her at the time. This became clear soon afterwards. She had days when she was more than usually affectionate with her mother and never left her skirts; but she could also be really naughty and irritable. On one of these bad days she tried to tip her little brother out of the pram. Her mother scolded her, whereupon she set up a loud wailing. Suddenly, in the midst of her tears, she said, "I don't know anything about where children come from!" She was then given the same explanation that her elder sister had received earlier. This seemed to allay the problem for her, and for several months there was peace. Then once more there were days when she was whining and bad-tempered. One day, quite out of the blue, she turned to her mother with the question "Was Freddie really in your inside?"

Mother: "Yes."

Sophie: "Did you push him out?"

Mother: "Yes."

Anna (butting in): "But was it down below?"

67   Here Anna employed a childish term which is used for the genitals as well as for the anus.

Sophie: "And then you let him drop down?"

68   The expression "drop down" comes from that toilet mechanism, of such absorbing interest to children, whereby one lets the excreta drop down into the bowl.

Anna: "Or was he sicked up?"

69   The evening before, Anna had been sick owing to a slightly upset stomach.

70   After a pause of several months Sophie had suddenly caught up and now wished to make sure of the explanation previously vouchsafed to her. This making doubly sure seems to indicate that doubts had arisen concerning the explanation given by her mother. To judge by the content of the questions, the doubts

146

arose because the process of birth had not been adequately explained. "Push" is a word children sometimes use for the act of defecation. It tells us along what lines the theory will develop with Sophie, too. Her further remark, as to whether one had let Freddie "drop down," betrays such a complete identification of her baby brother with excrement that it borders on the ludicrous. To this Anna makes the singular remark that perhaps Freddie was "sicked up." Her own vomiting of the day before had made a deep impression on her. It was the first time she had been sick since her earliest childhood. That was one way in which things could leave the body, though she had obviously not given it serious thought until now. (Only once had it occurred to her, and that was when they were discussing the body openings and she had thought of the mouth.) Her remark is a firm pointer away from the excrement theory. Why did she not point at once to the genitals? Her last dream gives us a clue to the probable reasons: there is something about the genitals which Anna still does not understand; something or other has to be done there to make it "work." Maybe it wasn't the genitals at all; maybe the seed for little children got into the body through the mouth, like food, and the child came out like "sick."

71   The detailed mechanism of birth, therefore, was still puzzling. Anna was again told by her mother that the child really does come out down below. About a month later, Anna suddenly had the following dream: *"I dreamt I was in the bedroom of Uncle and Auntie. Both of them were in bed. I pulled the bedclothes off Uncle, lay on his stomach, and joggled up and down on it."*

72   This dream came like a bolt from the blue. The children were then on holiday for several weeks and the father, who had been detained in town on business, had arrived on that same day for a visit. Anna was especially affectionate with him. He asked her jokingly, "Will you travel up to town with me this evening?" Anna: "Yes, and then I can sleep with you?" All this time she hung lovingly on her father's arm as her mother sometimes did. A few moments later she brought out her dream. Some days previously she had been staying as a guest with the aunt mentioned in the dream (the dream, too, was some days old). She had looked forward particularly to that visit, because

147

she was certain she would meet two small cousins—boys—in whom she showed an unfeigned interest. Unfortunately, the cousins were not there, and Anna was very disappointed. There must have been something in her present situation that was related to the content of the dream for it to be remembered so suddenly. The relation between the manifest content and the conversation with her father is clear enough. The uncle was a decrepit old gentleman and only known to the child from a few rare encounters. In the dream he is patently a substitute for her father. The dream itself creates a substitute for the disappointment of the day before: she is in bed with her father. Here we have the *tertium comparationis* with the present. Hence the sudden remembrance of the dream. The dream recapitulates a game which Anna often played in her father's (empty) bed, the game of joggling about and kicking with her legs on the mattress. From this game stemmed the question "Is this what Papa does?" Her immediate disappointment is that her father answered her question with the words, "You can sleep by yourself in the next room." Then follows the remembrance of the same dream which has already consoled her for a previous erotic disappointment (with the cousins). At the same time the dream is essentially an illustration of the theory that "it" takes place in bed, and by means of the aforementioned rhythmical movements. Whether the remark that she lay on her uncle's stomach had anything to do with her being sick cannot be proved.

73   Such is the extent of our observations up to the present. Anna is now a little over five years old and already in possession, as we have seen, of a number of the most important sexual facts. Any adverse effect of this knowledge upon her morals and character has yet to be observed. Of the favourable therapeutic effect we have spoken already. It is also quite clear from the report that the younger sister is in need of a special explanation for herself, as and when the problem arises for her. If the time is not ripe, no amount of enlightenment, it would seem, is of the slightest use.

74   I am no apostle of sex education for schoolchildren, or indeed of any standardized mechanical explanations. I am therefore not in a position to offer any positive and uniformly valid advice. I can only draw one conclusion from the material here recorded, which is, that we should try to see children as they

really are, and not as we would wish them; that, in educating them, we should follow the natural path of development, and eschew dead prescriptions.

Supplement

75   As already mentioned in the foreword, our views have undergone a considerable change since this paper was first published. There is, in the observations, one point in particular which has not been sufficiently appreciated, namely the fact that again and again, despite the enlightenment they received, the children exhibited a distinct preference for some fantastic explanation. Since the first appearance of the present work this tendency, contrary to my expectations, has increased: the children continue to favour a fantastic theory. In this matter I have before me a number of incontestable observations, some of them concerning the children of other parents. The four-year-old daughter of one of my friends, for instance, who does not hold with useless secrecy in education, was allowed last year to help her mother decorate the Christmas tree. But this year the child told her mother, "It wasn't right last year. This time I'll not look and you will lock the door with the key."

76   As a result of this and similar observations, I have been left wondering whether the fantastic or mythological explanation preferred by the child might not, for that very reason, be more suitable than a "scientific" one, which, although factually correct, threatens to clamp down the latch on fantasy for good. In the present instance the latch could be unclamped again, but only because the fantasy brushed "science" aside.

77   Did their enlightenment harm the children? Nothing of the sort was observed. They developed healthily and normally. The problems they broached apparently sank right into the background, presumably as a result of the manifold external interests arising out of school life, and the like. The fantasy activity was not harmed in the least, nor did it pursue paths that could be described as in any way abnormal. Occasional remarks or observations of a delicate nature were made openly and without secrecy.

78   I have therefore come to hold the view that the earlier free

discussions took the wind out of the children's imagination and thus prevented any secretive fantasy from developing which would have cast a sidelong glance at these things, and would, in consequence, have been nothing but an obstacle to the free development of thinking. The fact that the fantasy activity simply ignored the right explanation seems, in my view, to be an important indication that all freely developing thought has an irresistible need to emancipate itself from the realism of fact and to create a world of its own.

79   Consequently, however little advisable it is to give children false explanations which would only sow the seeds of mistrust, it is, so it seems to me, no less inadvisable to insist on the acceptance of the right explanation. For the freedom of the mind's development would merely be suppressed through such rigid consistency, and the child forced into a concretism of outlook that would preclude further development. Side by side with the biological, the spiritual, too, has its inviolable rights. It is assuredly no accident that primitive peoples, even in adult life, make the most fantastic assertions about well-known sexual processes, as for instance that coitus has nothing to do with pregnancy.[10] From this it has been concluded that these people do not even know there is such a connection. But more accurate investigation has shown that they know very well that with animals copulation is followed by pregnancy. Only for human beings is it denied—not *not known,* but flatly *denied*—that this is so, for the simple reason that they prefer a mythological explanation which has freed itself from the trammels of concretism. It is not hard to see that in these facts, so frequently observed among primitives, there lie the beginnings of *abstraction,* which is so very important for culture. We have every reason to suppose that this is also true of the psychology of the child. If certain South American Indians really and truly call themselves red cockatoos and expressly repudiate a figurative interpretation of this fact, this has absolutely nothing to do with any sexual repression on "moral" grounds, but is due to the law of independence inherent in the thinking function and to its emancipation from the concretism of sensuous perceptions. We

---

[10] [Cf. Bronislaw Malinowski, *The Sexual Life of Savages* (3rd edn., London and New York, 1932).—EDITORS.]

must assign a separate principle to the thinking function, a principle which coincides with the beginnings of sexuality only in the polyvalent germinal disposition of the very young child. To reduce the origins of thinking to mere sexuality is an undertaking that runs counter to the basic facts of human psychology.

BIBLIOGRAPHY

BIBLIOGRAPHY

A. LIST OF PERIODICALS CITED, WITH ABBREVIATIONS

Allg. Z. Psychiat. = *Allgemeine Zeitschrift für Psychiatrie und psychisch-gerichtliche Medizin.* Berlin.

Amer. J. Psychol. = *American Journal of Psychology.* Baltimore.

Arch. ges. Psychol. = *Archiv für die gesamte Psychologie.* Leipzig.

Arch. Kriminalanthrop. = *Archiv für Kriminalanthropologie und Kriminalistik.* Leipzig.

Arch. Rass. u. GesBiol. = *Archiv für Rassen- und Gesellschaftsbiologie.* Leipzig and Berlin.

J. abnorm. Psychol. = *Journal of Abnormal Psychology.* Boston.

Jb. psychoanal. psychopath. Forsch. = *Jahrbuch für psychoanalytische und psychopathologische Forschungen.* Vienna and Leipzig.

J. Psychol. Neurol. = *Journal für Psychologie und Neurologie.* Leipzig.

Münch. med. Wschr. = *Münchener medizinische Wochenschrift.* Munich.

Psychiat.-neurol. Wschr. = *Psychiatrisch-neurologische Wochenschrift.* Halle.

Z. ReligPsychol. = *Zeitschrift für Religionspsychologie.* Halle.

Z. ges. Strafrechtswiss. = *Zeitschrift für die gesamte Strafrechtswissenschaft.* Berlin.

Zbl. Nervenheilk. = *Zentralblatt für Nervenheilkunde und Psychiatrie.* Berlin.

Zbl. Psychoan. = *Zentralblatt für Psychoanalyse.* Wiesbaden.

B. GENERAL BIBLIOGRAPHY

ASCHAFFENBURG, GUSTAV. "Die Beziehungen des sexuellen Lebens zur Entstehung von Nerven- und Geisteskrankheiten," *Münch. med. Wschr.*, LIII (1906), 1793–98.

BINSWANGER, LUDWIG. "Freud'sche Mechanismen in der Symptomatologie von Psychosen," *Psychiat.-neurol. Wschr.*, VIII (1906).

BLEULER, EUGEN. "Consciousness and Association." In: JUNG, *Studies in Word-Association* (1918), pp. 266–96. (Orig. 1905).

———. "Die Psychoanalyse Freuds," *Jb. psychoanal. psychopath. Forsch.*, II (1910), 623–730.

———. "Versuch einer naturwissenschaftlichen Betrachtung der psychologischen Grundbegriffe," *Allg. Z. Psychiat.*, L (1894), 133–68.

BREUER, JOSEF, and FREUD, SIGMUND. *Studies on Hysteria.* Translated by James and Alix Strachey. (Complete Psychological Works of Sigmund Freud, Standard Edition, 2.) London, 1955. (Original: *Studien über Hysterie.* 1895.)

FREUD, SIGMUND. "Five Lectures on Psycho-Analysis." (Delivered on the Occasion of the Celebration of the Twentieth Anniversary of the Foundation of Clark University, Worcester, Mass., September 1909.) Translated by James Strachey. In: Standard Edn.,* 11. 1957. (Original: *Ueber Psychoanalyse.* 1910.)

———. "Fragment of an Analysis of a Case of Hysteria." Translated by Alix and James Strachey. Standard Edn.,* 7. (Orig.: "Bruchstück einer Hysterie-Analyse," 1905.)

———. "Obsessive Acts and Religious Practices." Translated by R. C. McWatters. In: Standard Edn.,* 9. 1959. (Original: "Zwangshandlungen und Religionsübung," *Z. ReligPsychol.*, I (1907).)

FÜRST, EMMA. "Statistical Investigations on Word-Associations and on Familial Agreement in Reaction Type among Uneducated Persons." In: C. G. JUNG (ed.). *Studies in Word-Association.* Translated by M. D. Eder. London, 1918; New York, 1919.

GOETHE, JOHANN WOLFGANG VON. *Faust: Part One.* Translated by Philip Wayne. (Penguin Classics.) Harmondsworth, 1956.

GRABOWSKY, ADOLF. "Psychologische Tatbestandsdiagnostik," *Beilage zur Allgemeine Zeitung* (Tübingen), 15 Dec. 1905.

GROSS, ALFRED. "Die Assoziationsmethode im Strafprozess," *Z. ges. Strafrechtswiss.*, XXVI (1906), 19–40.

GROSS, HANS. "Zur psychologischen Tatbestandsdiagnostik," *Arch. Kriminalanthrop.*, XIX (1905), 49–59.

HASLEBACHER, J. A., "Psychoneurosen und Psychoanalyse," *Correspondenzblatt für Schweizer Ärzte* (Basel), XL:7 (Mar. 1, 1910).

HORACE. *Satires, Epistles, and Ars Poetica.* With an English transla-

* The Standard Edition of the Complete Psychological Works of Sigmund Freud, translated under the general editorship of James Strachey. London.

tion by H. Rushton Fairclough. (Loeb Classical Library.) London and New York, 1929.

JONES, ERNEST. *Sigmund Freud: Life and Work.* London, 1953–57. 3 vols. (Also pub. New York separately. Refs. are to the London edn.)

JÖRGER, J. "Die Familie Zero," *Arch. Rass. u. GesBiol.* (Leipzig and Berlin), II (1905), 494–559.

JUNG, CARL GUSTAV. "The Association Method." In: *Experimental Researches.* Collected Works, 2.

———. *Collected Papers on Analytical Psychology.* Edited by Constance Long, translated by various persons. London and New York, 1916; 2nd edn., 1917.

———. "New Paths in Psychology." In: *Two Essays on Analytical Psychology.* Collected Works, 7.

———. "On the Psychology and Pathology of So-Called Occult Phenomena." In: *Psychiatric Studies.* Collected Works, 1.

———. "Psychological Aspects of the Mother Archetype." In: *The Archetypes and the Collective Unconscious.* Collected Works, 9, i.

———. *Psychology and Alchemy.* Collected Works, 12.

———. "The Psychology of Dementia Praecox." In: *The Psychogenesis of Mental Disease.* Collected Works, 3.

———, ed. *Studies in Word-Association.* Translated by M. D. Eder. London and New York, 1918.

———. *Wandlungen und Symbole der Libido.* Leipzig and Vienna, 1912.

KRAFFT-EBING, RICHARD VON. *Psychopathia Sexualis.* Translated by F. J. Rebman. London, 1901. (Orig. 1886.)

PRINCE, MORTON. "The Mechanism and Interpretation of Dreams," *J. abnorm. Psychol.,* V (1910–11), 139–95.

PUTNAM, JAMES J. "Personal Impressions of Sigmund Freud and His Work, with special reference to His Recent Lectures at Clark University," *J. abnorm. Psychol.,* IV (1909–10), 293, 372.

———. "Persönliche Erfahrungen mit Freud's psychoanalytischer Methode," *Zbl. Psychoan.,* I (1910–11), 533–48.

RIKLIN, FRANZ. *Wish Fulfilment and Symbolism in Fairy Tales.* Translated by William A. White. New York, 1915. (Orig.: *Wunscherfüllung und Symbolik im Märchen,* 1908.)

SCHOPENHAUER, ARTHUR. *Transcendent Speculations on the Apparent Design in the Fate of the Individual.* Translated by David

Irvine. London, 1913. (Original: "Über die anscheinende Absichtlichkeit im Schicksale des Einzelnen," *Sämmtliche Werke*, ed. Julius Frauenstadt, 2nd edn., Leipzig, 1877, Vol. V [*Parerga und Paralipomena*, Vol. II], 222–23.)

SOMMER, ROBERT. *Familienforschung und Vererbungslehre*. Leipzig, 1907.

VIGOUROUX, A., and JUQUELIER, P. *La Contagion mentale*. (Bibliothèque internationale de psychologie.) Paris, 1904.

WERTHEIMER, MAX. "Experimentelle Untersuchungen zur Tatbestandsdiagnostik," *Arch. ges. Psychol.*, VI (1905–6), 59–131.

———, and KLEIN, JULIUS. "Psychologische Tatbestandsdiagnostik," *Arch. Kriminalanthrop.*, XV (1904), 72–113.

ZIERMER, MANFRED. "Genealogische Studien über die Vererbung geistiger Eigenschaften," *Arch. Rass.- u. GesBiol.*, V (1908), 178–220, 327–63.

INDEX

INDEX

A

abasia, 35
abreaction, 41, 44
abstraction, 150
Adler, Alfred, 119, 129n
adolescence: introversion in, 129
affection, rivalry in, 129
affects: aetiological significance in hysteria, 40f; blocking of, 42; displacement of, 43; effects of traumatic, 42f; in normal persons, 41
ambivalence: of father-imago, 114
Amsterdam Congress (1907), 110n
anal eroticism, 50, 51, 88
analogies, thinking in, 140
analyst: attitude of, 4f, 19; fear of loss of, 75; *see also* transference
Andermatt, 55ff
angel(s), 140; children as, 125f, 136, 144
animal(s), little, dream of, 137f
Anna, *see* Jung, Carl Gustav, CASES IN SUMMARY
ant, queen, 108
aphonia, 35, 81, 82
archetype, 108f, 115f, 126; of father, 114, 115
Aschaffenburg, Gustav, 33ff, 40n, 97
Asmodeus, 115, 116n
association(s): chains of, and complex, 46; and dreams, 47; free, 4, 19, 45, 70f
association experiments (association method), and families, 97; and psychoanalysis, 3-32; 37
attitude: and reaction-type, 98
attributes, personification of, 60f

aufsitzen, 58n, 67n
automatisms, unconscious psychic, and hysteria, 40
automatons, children treated as, 130
auto-suggestion, 36f

B

barn, 55ff
bathing place, 55ff
"big brother" fantasy, 136, 143
Binet, Alfred, 69
Binswanger, Ludwig, 40 & n
Binswanger, Otto, 72
biological and spiritual: respective rights of, 150
bird(s), 108, 114
birth, 127; Anna's reaction to, 128; child's idea of, 125ff, 128n, 131-136, 140f, 144f, 146, 147; inadequately explained, 147; *see also* stork theory
black man (dream-symbol), 111f
bladder, irritation of, and dreams, 111
Bleuler, Paul Eugen, 5, 60, 69, 70n
"blinded," 82f, 84
blinding, 112
brain, ectoderm and, 121
Breuer, Josef, 3, 40, 41; "Anna O." case, 41; *Studies on Hysteria*, 41, 42n
Brill, A. A., 68, 116n
brother, 136; *see also* "big brother" fantasy

C

Caesarian section, 134
cases, *see under* Jung, Carl Gustav

Jörger, J., 96*n*
Journal of Abnormal Psychology, 69
Judaism, 113*n*
Jung, Carl Gustav:
CASES IN SUMMARY (*in order of presentation, numbered for reference*):
[1] Woman, 55, with climacteric neurosis, illustrating search for father-substitute in unsatisfactory marriage.—99*ff*
[2] Man, 34, with nervous stomach trouble, illustrating effect of masochistic-homosexual relationship to father.—101*ff*
[3] Woman, 36, with anxiety, depression, and guilt-feeling for marrying against father's will.—103*ff*
[4] Boy, 8, enuretic, illustrating overdependence on mother and fear of father.—110*ff*
[5] Anna, aged 3, subject of "Psychic Conflicts in a Child."—125-151
[6] Girl, aged 15, who harboured an unconscious fantasy of mother's death.—127
WORKS: "Association, Dream, and Hysterical Symptoms," 82*n*; "The Association Method," 69*n*; *Collected Papers on Analytical Psychology*, 55*n*, 69*n*, 94*n*; *Diagnostische Assoziationsstudien*, 37*n*; *Experimental Researches*, 37*n*, 82*n*; "New Paths in Psychology," 91*n*; "On the Psychology and Pathology of So-called Occult Phenomena," 24*n*; "Psychic Conflicts in a Child," 66*n*, 69*n*; "Psychoanalyse und Assoziationsexperiment," 37*n*; "Psychoanalysis and Association Experiments," 37*n*; "Psychological Aspects of the Mother Archetype," 96*n*; *Psychology and Alchemy*, 115*n*; "The Psychology of Dementia Praecox," 60*n*, 135*n*; *Studies in Word Association*, 37*n*; *Symbols of Transformation*, 53*n*, 80*n*, 94*n*, 96*n*; *Two Essays on Analytical*

Psychology, 91*n*; *Wandlungen und Symbole der Libido*, 80*n*, 92*n*, 94

K

Kepler, J., 39
"kill," 140; meaning to children, 126*f*
Klein, Julius, 5
knowledge: child's unnatural craving for, 133; fear and desire for, 133; thirst for, 138
Kraepelin, Emil, 9, 97
Krafft-Ebing, Richard von, 28*n*

L

lake, 55*ff*
libido, 48*f*, 91*f*, 96, 121; converted, fear as expression of, 133; investment of, 49; suspension as transference of, 129*n*
licentiousness, 91
"Little Hans," *see* "Hans, Little"
loneliness, 79
love, 113*n*; introverted, 129, 132; securing by force, 132; *see also* fear
Löwenfeld, Leopold, 5
lying, 130

M

maenads, 61
Malinowski, Bronislaw, 150*n*
Maria, Axiom of, 115*n*
masculinity, premature, 111
Mass, the, 113*n*
mass therapy, and psychoanalysis, 47
masturbation, 12, 14*f*, 18, 25, 27, 50, 51, 121, 134
Mendel, Kurt, 88
Messina, earthquake, 132*f*
method(s): Freudian, as auto-suggestion, 36*f*; —, development of, 44*f*; —, and hysteria, 35*f*; —, theoretical foundations, 45; psycho-biological, 119, 120; purely empirical, 87

Q

questions, children's, 128n, 131n, 132ff, 143f

R

Raguel, 114f, 116n
Raimann, Emil, 43 & n
Rascher's Yearbook, 91
reactions, value-predicate, 98
reaction-time, in psychoanalysis, 9
reaction-types, similarity in families, 97
realism, child's outgrowing of, 122
rebirth, archetype of, 126n; see also reincarnation
regression, 96
reincarnation theory, 126ff
relapse, 75f
relatives, and association reactions, 97
religion, 120; history of, and fantasies, 113n; infantile constellations and, 109n
reminiscences, 41, 44
repetition, in reactions, 11; significance of, 60
repression, 122, 129n; Freud's concept of, 3f; and hysteria, 49, 51; in hysteria, 3f; sexual, 150; sexual, God and, 114n
reproduction method, 5f
resistance(s), children's, 130, 132, 136; to complex, 46; to hysterical fantasies, 49; to wish-fulfilment, 80
revenge, 85
reveries, children's, 129, 132
Riklin, Franz, 5, 140n
rivalry: see affection
rose, 140
rumour, analysis by, 77n; psychology of, 55ff

S

Sadger, I., 88, 89
salvation, 112
Sara, 114f, 116n

satyrs, 61
Schiller, J.C.F. von, 126
schizophrenia, 60f
Schopenhauer, Arthur, 107n
Scripture, Edward Wheeler, 68
self-control, 91
self-knowledge, 70
sex, and Freudian psychology, 121; and infantile thinking, 120; sexual education, 148
sexuality: adult and infantile, compared, 120; fate of, and life's fate, 113n; and formation of psychoneuroses, 33ff, 43; Freud's concept, 48f; and Freud, 43f, 49, 88f; infantile, 123; a façon de parler, 123; and origins of thinking, 151; overdeveloped concept of, 123; and parental authority, 110; polymorphous, child's, 121f; and spiritual functions, 121; thinking function and, 121; see also hysteria
shame, 49, 51f
ship, see steamer
Sileni, 61
sin, original, 109n
snake, as dream symbol, 111f
Sommer, Robert, 96n
soul, naturally religious, 114
South America, Indians of, 150
speech, inhibition of, 111
Spielmeyer, Walter, 39
spiritual, function, 121; see also biological and spiritual
split personality, 24
splitting of consciousness, 41
spontaneous utterances, significance of child's, 130
stammerers, 129n
staying up late, of children, 137
steamer, 55ff
Steinthal, Heymann, 53
Stern, 65
stomach: fat, dream of, 139
stone(s), 76ff, 84
stork theory, 125f, 127f, 131f, 133f, 135f, 144

THE COLLECTED WORKS OF
C. G. JUNG

T HE PUBLICATION of the first complete edition, in English, of the works of C. G. Jung was undertaken by Routledge and Kegan Paul, Ltd., in England and by Bollingen Foundation in the United States. The American edition is number XX in Bollingen Series, which since 1967 has been published by Princeton University Press. The edition contains revised versions of works previously published, such as *Psychology of the Unconscious*, which is now entitled *Symbols of Transformation*; works originally written in English, such as *Psychology and Religion*; works not previously translated, such as *Aion*; and, in general, new translations of virtually all of Professor Jung's writings. Prior to his death, in 1961, the author supervised the textual revision, which in some cases is extensive. Sir Herbert Read (d. 1968), Dr. Michael Fordham, and Dr. Gerhard Adler compose the Editorial Committee; the translator is R. F. C. Hull (except for Volume 2) and William McGuire is executive editor.

The price of the volumes varies according to size; they are sold separately, and may also be obtained on standing order. Several of the volumes are extensively illustrated. Each volume contains an index and in most a bibliography; the final volume will contain a complete bibliography of Professor Jung's writings and a general index to the entire edition.

In the following list, dates of original publication are given in parentheses (of original composition, in brackets). Multiple dates indicate revisions.

* Published 1957; 2nd edn., 1970.

* Published 1960.   † Published 1961.
‡ Published 1956; 2nd edn., 1967. (65 plates, 43 text figures.)

---

* Published 1971.   † Published 1953; 2nd edn., 1966.
‡ Published 1960; 2nd edn., 1969.

* Published 1959; 2nd edn., 1968. (Part I: 79 plates, with 29 in colour.)

* Published 1964; 2nd edn., 1970. (8 plates.)
† Published 1958; 2nd edn., 1969.

* Published 1953; 2nd edn., completely revised, 1968. (270 illustrations.)
† Published 1968. (50 plates, 4 text figures.)
‡ Published 1963; 2nd edn., 1970. (10 plates.)

* Published 1966.
† Published 1954; 2nd edn., revised and augmented, 1966. (13 illustrations.)
‡ Published 1954.

The Development of Personality (1934)
Marriage as a Psychological Relationship (1925)

18. MISCELLANY
Posthumous and Other Miscellaneous Works

19. BIBLIOGRAPHY AND INDEX
Complete Bibliography of C. G. Jung's Writings
General Index to the Collected Works

See also:

C. G. JUNG: LETTERS

Selected and edited by Gerhard Adler, in collaboration with Aniela Jaffé.
Translations from the German by R.F.C. Hull.

VOL. 1: 1906–1950*
VOL. 2: 1951–1961

* Published 1973. In the Princeton edition, the *Letters* constitute Bollingen
Series XCV.

†THE FREUD/JUNG LETTERS

The Correspondence between Sigmund Freud and C. G. Jung
Translated by Ralph Manheim and R.F.C. Hull
Edited by William McGuire

†Published 1974. In the Princeton edition, *The Freud/Jung Letters* constitutes
Bollingen Series XCIV.

Also available in Princeton/Bollingen Paperbacks